Up, Up, Up and away holiday club

A five-day programme for 5-11 year olds

Captain Alan Price CA with Liz Lunn

kevin
mayhew

First published in 2003 by
KEVIN MAYHEW LTD
Buxhall, Stowmarket, Suffolk, IP14 3BW
E-mail: info@kevinmayhewltd.com
KINGSGATE PUBLISHING INC
1000 Pannell Street, Suite G, Columbia, MO 65201
E-mail: sales@kingsgatepublishing.com

9 8 7 6 5 4 3 2 1 0

ISBN 1 84417 065 9
Catalogue No 1500584

Illustrated by Steve English
Cover design by Angela Selfe
Edited by Elisabeth Bates
Typesetting by Richard Weaver

Printed and bound in Great Britain

Contents

Introduction

Whatever reasons you may have for running a holiday club, this material is designed to help you in your task. The background theme of aeroplanes is a popular one, appealing to both sexes, and provides plenty of inspiration for room decoration etc. The approach is essentially a thematic one and deals with discipleship issues as well as those of basic faith. Thus there is something of interest both to the Christian child as well as one with little previous experience. This package is not designed with the completely unchurched child in mind, and some assumptions of prior knowledge are made. Those who give the main teaching will need to be flexible and ready to make some adjustments if it becomes evident that a substantial number of children attending need every basic truth explained in detail.

Christian children need the extra stimulus that a holiday club can give. Rather than just being amongst the subjects of our mission, in many ways they are also our fellow team members, as they share what they know with others who don't. There is a distinct emphasis in this material to encourage them to be witnesses of their faith.

Eighty-four per cent of British children have no meaningful contact with the Church. Many find the step into a church building too big to take. A holiday club gives some the chance to 'taste and see'. They meet adults and children who know God in some way. If the event is in neutral premises, it is even less 'threatening'. In a light way, they can be introduced to the good news of Jesus and what he offers – and what he asks of those who follow him.

Children and the Kingdom of God

Our aim for children is to give them the dignity of knowing who they are in Christ, and to give them a taste of what God has for them now, not just in the future.

We need to have a thorough grasp of the place of children in the Kingdom of God. More than 50 years ago someone wrote,

> In general, children are told they must wait and prepare themselves before they can fulfil life's big responsibilities. But Jesus needs them now, and they need him, and can be as real and true Christians as grown-up people. (*Towards the Conversion of England*, 1948)

We need to have a wide view of evangelism and children, by examining how a child comes to faith. There is little specifically about children in the New Testament. Perhaps we should simply look at Jesus' attitude to children – his evangelistic method. He never dismissed them; rather he welcomed them – hugged them – honoured them – gave them dignity. At one point he even suggested that God revealed things to them that the wise and learned could not perceive (see Matthew 11:20-26).

There is one particular meeting between Jesus and children mentioned by each of the synoptic writers, when children were brought to him and he compared them to those seeking the Kingdom of God (Matthew 19:13; Mark 10:13; Luke 18:1).

But was it more than comparison? What was Jesus saying about children? Jesus proclaimed the gospel 'of the Kingdom of God'. In his many statements we understand he was speaking not so much of a geographical kingdom, but rather of the reign of God, and he frequently linked it with himself (e.g. Luke 11:20). Ron Buckland concludes this:

> When Jesus says that the kingdom of God belongs to children, he is saying that children belong to him. He embodies the kingdom . . . (*Perspectives on Children and the Gospel*, Scripture Union, 2001.)

Yet we must weigh this against the scriptural teaching about sin. Children do not sin like adults, and to treat them as if they do raises all kinds of complications. Yet children are sinners like the rest of us, and repentance is needed by all who would follow Jesus. They might not be thieves and robbers, or guilty of horrors that make newspaper headlines, but 'Ordinary sin is as deadly as the more dramatic sort' (John Inchley). Jesus died on the cross for ordinary children, too!

All children begin with God but will drift from that position unless an effective nurturing or evangelistic influence operates in their lives.

Children of Christian parents, or children who have some other significant Christian person (Sunday-school teacher, or godparent, perhaps) may not be 'lost' and cut off from God in the same way as a child who has been brought up in a godless situation.

Children generally do not make a rational decision by weighing up the claims of Christ and deciding for him. Although that may be part of the journey of faith, most children (and adults) see a group of people they like. When they realise that Jesus is the one who makes the group so good, they want to join and have Jesus as their friend too.

Salvation is a process, not an event. The children attending the holiday club will be at various stages in that process or journey. This is important in two ways.

Firstly, it is often the sum total of the holiday club that will bring a child nearer to God rather than any one part of it. Thus it is near the end of the event that we often see a child begin to respond.

Secondly, as learning and growth is a process, it is appropriate in the holiday club to give children opportunities to make their appropriate response to whatever they are learning about God and/or about themselves.

The important question, therefore, is *not* 'Have you made/When did you make a commitment to Christ?' It is more important for each child to know where they are *now* with Jesus. Do they know they belong to him? Do they feel there is anything missing in their friendship with him? It may then be appropriate to ask if they have ever made a definite step of saying 'yes' to God, without necessarily implying that if they have not made such a conscious act they are not a Christian! (That may be true, but not necessarily!)

For some, therefore, it will be a first step, whilst for others it will be a further step of faith. For some it will be a different kind of response. We need to be sensitive and flexible! Wherever they are in the journey of faith, we want to enable them to move on. Ensure that there is a supply of suitable booklets explaining the basic Gospel message that will help clarify the process of becoming Christian.

Empowering children

As has been said earlier, this material touches on discipleship issues, such as experiencing the power of the Holy Spirit, which St Peter said was for 'you and your children' (Acts 2:39). It contains encouragement for children to take seriously their role as witnesses for Christ – in telling their own story as well as being able to tell the story of Jesus; in demonstrating God's love by what they do, as well as by what they say. The writers of this material believe that there is a role for children now, not just when they are older. Adults should not forget the number of times that Jesus Christ said we should be like children!

The 'take off with Jesus' theme

The Good News of the Kingdom is not just about the death and resurrection of the Lord Jesus Christ – it is wider than that, but the story of Jesus is essential for a true understanding of the Gospel message. Thus, this material deals with that essential message, but also deals with wider discipleship issues. We use the concept of the Kingdom of God – the term Jesus himself used in describing the Good News. Whilst it is impossible to deal with every issue concerning the Kingdom, we have chosen fundamental themes to help boys and girls to know Jesus better, and to know how to be his friends. It is pertinent to the children wherever they are on the journey of faith.

There is a sense that when they discover that following Jesus is an adventure, they 'take off'. The aeroplane background theme is one that appeals to both sexes and all ages, and gives much scope for decoration of the venue.

Practical tips for organising the event

Running a holiday club is great fun but it needs careful and prayerful planning. It can involve many people of all ages in your church fellowship as helpers, but you need one or two people to take overall responsibility to make sure the thing happens. Here are some suggested steps to help you.

Step 1

Prayer Meet as a church or group of children's leaders to pray asking for guidance. You may consider gathering the Christian children to do the same, or ask them to pray at home and tell you what they feel God has said in response to their prayers. (Whilst these children may be the recipients of our efforts, they are also our main recruiting agents – and even the best evangelists.) Is it right to hold a holiday club? Who is it for? What is the aim? When? Where? Who will help? How do we do it? Once you embark on this venture arrange regular prayer times to support it; there will be people who are willing to pray even if they are not able to be involved in the actual week. What about a budget? Will the church finance the event, or will fundraising and/or admission fees be required?

Setting the target Deciding the aim of the event is crucial. Just to run the club is not a particularly good aim in itself. Are you aiming to reach unchurched children? Do you want to build on contacts made in the local school? Do you want to have a special time of encouragement for your regular children? Or are you wanting to offer child minding facilities for the community? Each of these is valid, and your aim may be a combination of two or more of these. Whatever is decided must be accepted by all involved – including the church leadership.

Step 2

The venue This depends a little on the kind of event you are planning – its size, the number of separate meeting places required for simultaneous activities, etc. Personally, during all-together times I prefer children to sit on the floor, rather than on chairs (the latter seem to restrict the children in their enthusiasm and their movement in worship). For this reason the floor needs to be in reasonable condition. School buildings are generally ideal, with the added bonus that they are 'neutral' venues – particularly valuable when reaching unchurched children, or if it is an inter-church event. Check whether you are insured for the venue/occasion.

Other important considerations are: *Safety* – does the venue have controlled access, to ensure children are safe from those who might wander in off the street, and to prevent children from wandering off unnoticed? Is it secure enough for equipment to be left on site? Does it comply with health and safety requirements as far as toilets and food preparation (if appropriate) are concerned?

Play space – is there adequate space for the number of expected children indoors as well as out of doors?

Step 3

Team You will need a lot of people!! It's difficult to give a minimum number because so much depends on the number of children. You need to be discerning about who comes on team and everyone needs to sign a declaration for the Children's Act 1989 (see Appendix). Often people will help with a holiday club who would not normally do children's work. Your denominational headquarters (Diocesan Office etc.) will have a Child Protection Policy which you should follow in order to honour and protect the children in your care. Secondary School-age children involved in the church (Pathfinder age and Youth Club) can be helpful 'extra' leaders to work alongside your adults. The main requirement of team members is that they have some clear Christian commitment. During the event, team members need to wear something that easily identifies them as such – a badge, a sash, a tabard or even a specially printed T-shirt, etc.
You will need the following helpers:

- One or two people leading up front, preferably the same people each day for continuity

- Musicians

- PA operator who may also be responsible for playing backing tracks if no musicians are available

- A group leader for each small group. I usually reckon on 8-10 children maximum per group so if you have 10 groups you need 10 people! An additional helper per group is a bonus, and enables the group to be more effective.

- A co-ordinator of the craft

- A games organiser

- Someone to register and welcome the children

- Someone to do refreshments

- A publicity co-ordinator/designer

- Artists to make the set and props

- Actors for the drama, or puppeteers

- Stewards to act as security on the door, and generally helping with practical things

- A treasurer, unless the church treasurer is happy to handle this

Find out who is willing to help and when you meet to plan the event you can distribute tasks. People can do more than one task, e.g. the people who register could also do refreshments, the publicity is done beforehand so that person can do something during the event. Many can help make the props or puppets! During the actual week small-group leaders need to focus on that task because they need to be available to welcome the children into the groups as they arrive, and they stay with their group for the whole morning.

Step 4

Planning You need to decide how you are going to use the material in this book. The leader(s) should be familiar with the material and then meet with key people initially to work out what is involved, and then have a planning session for everyone. Decide how long the event will be, five or three days (which three?) and the timing of each day, whether it is morning or afternoon. You need to plan:

- Distribution of tasks – who does what and when

- The stage, if there is none in the venue. When everyone is standing, the leader must still be seen. In some cases, additional lighting may be required

- Amplification (PA) – sufficient to enable the leader, the actors/puppeteers (and musicians) to be heard

- Actors or puppeteers – including a producer who will be responsible for rehearsals as well as the performances

- Making the set (see Production notes, p.130), props or puppets and puppet theatre – with reference to the producer

- The music, including rehearsal times and the words for children to use (see Notes about music, p.19)

- The craft – obtaining materials and equipment required

- The games – obtaining equipment required

- Refreshments, bearing in mind any known food allergies etc.

- Administration tasks such as photocopying the registration forms and worksheets

- Small-group time and training sessions for small-group leaders

- Decoration of the main venue (The Runway) and the 'Hangars'

- Publicity

- Prayer-support schedule

- Family Service

- Follow-up – what further contact will there be for children who attend the event?

Step 5

Publicity This is important; it is helpful to have a co-ordinator. In these days of desk-top publishing on home computers, it is not difficult to produce good publicity. Go for as much colour as possible within your budget. Some may prefer to find publicity items suitable for over-printing from organisations such as Christian Publicity Organisation (CPO). According to your aim(s) use the contacts you have, such as midweek clubs, local schools and Sunday groups. Most shops and libraries will be willing to display posters and schools will give out invitations. (Ensure you provide sufficient copies.) If you have an opportunity to take an assembly, then use that time to advertise the club. Whilst advance warning is essential to ensure parents don't plan alternative activities, in general, the posters need to go out about 3 weeks before and the invitations about 10-14 days before. A last-minute reminder just before the event is always a good idea.

Step 6

Organisation This material is written for 5-11 year olds, and organised into two age groups, 5-7, 8-11. If numbers dictate (and resources permit) you could have three age-groups: 5-6, 7-8, 9-11, in which case you will need to adapt the worksheets and teaching material and have an additional colour (blue?). Have everything prepared before the week starts (see Planning). The next section gives you the programme for each day.

- Allow time the day/evening before to get the church/hall ready and decorated

- Pray: before you start the day gather the team to pray and share God's word. Ask the team to arrive at least an hour before, to allow time to set up, to worship and pray, and to go through the programme

- Register the children on arrival (see form at end of this section). It is important to get a contact phone number and to know who is collecting them. Each child will join a small group for the whole event, with the same group leader. On Day 1 you can put them into their small groups as they register, making sure that you even out the groups. The children can choose which small group they join, up to the required number, but you may need to be more flexible about relative sizes of groups. Register new children daily, and record the attendance of every child

- The first thing the children do is to go to small groups (called 'hangars' in this programme) where they meet the leader and do whatever 'flight preparation' activity is planned for that day. Such 'flight preparation activities' are intended to build relationships, and could include:

  - Badge making – especially useful on Day 1

  - Decorating the hangars – giving the space a group identity

  - Making an aeroplane collage or a model airport out of scrap materials; this could last over several days and be an inter-group competition

  - Talk about the previous day's teaching and/or worksheets

- It is helpful to have assistant leaders attached to each small group. Some children need help writing or doing craft, and taking to the toilet. Each child should have a name badge, which may be handed in at the end of each day for safe keeping, until the last day.

- The children are divided into age groups (Green and Red) and into teams (Helicopters and Jets, or Balloons and Gliders, etc.). The small groups are therefore called Green Jets 1, 2, 3 etc., Green Helicopters 1, 2, 3, etc. for 5-7s, and Red Jets 1, 2, 3, etc. for 8-11s. Arrange your hall/church so that the Jets' Hangars are down one side and the Helicopters' Hangars the other side with the Green groups at the front. You can challenge the groups to decorate their hangars appropriately. Travel agents and even airports have all sorts of posters and publicity leaflets that you could acquire.

- The programme starts with 'The Runway' – a time together after the Flight Preparation activity. Then there are three sessions which the children rotate round by age group: craft, small-group teaching, games. There is also a break for refreshments.

  How you organise this will depend on your space. If you are limited to two areas only, everyone could do small-group time, then have craft in one area and games in the other. If you only have a hall available, then you keep the children all together and all do craft, games, small groups in rotation. This would be difficult but not impossible, especially if you put a limit on numbers.

- During 'The Runway' encourage the children to sit in their teams, Jets and Helicopters. It is helpful if the leaders sit amongst them to encourage them to listen and take part. One of the items you may like to include is AIR TRAFFIC CONTROL. This is a competition between Jets and Helicopters. At a given signal (a whistle or chime) the children have to stand up and be very still. The quickest team wins.

- There is a scoreboard in the style of a flight-path (see Acetate master 3). After the signal each team gets 3 points and moves on 3 spaces. In addition the winning team has the opportunity to get more points (travel more spaces). To do this you either use a spinning device, or pull a ball out of a bag for a choice of circle, diamond, square or star. On cards with the matching shapes drawn on the reverse side, there are instructions which will either take them forward, back or leave them where they are. Circles are generally 'good', diamonds are 'risky', and squares are 'dangerous'. The star cards have a forfeit for one of the leaders from that side which may earn the team extra 'air miles' (see Appendix 2).

- Small-group leaders are very important. They remain with their groups all the time and really get to know the children. They take them to each activity so they need to know exactly what their group is doing each day; they help the group with both craft and games. During the refreshments break they need to serve their group with drinks and snacks, etc. They also lead the small-group teaching and some train-ing for this will be helpful. Small-group leaders have a modelling role, especially during The Runway. The children will take their cue from their leader about actions in songs, how and when to pray, focusing on the stage and general behaviour. It is much easier for a group leader sitting amongst the children to halt a conversation (or a fight) before it develops, and redirect attention back to the stage.

- *Craft* There are suggestions for each day for both age groups. You could have one activity for all the children each day which you obviously change for the next day. Alternatively, you could have 5 activities repeated daily and around which the groups rotate through the week. See Craft sessions, page 84.

- *Games* There are different ideas for games for each day. This is an opportunity for unusual games, but younger children especially enjoy familiar games. You may want to repeat whichever games you find work well.

- *Final Runway* It is important that you end each day's session properly so encourage your team to keep to time and make sure you come together at the end to finish off. It is helpful to have people (such as the stewards) welcoming parents who come to collect, chatting, explaining the morning and especially watching that no child goes out on their own without an adult. This is the time to give out invitations to the Family Service and any other family activity you may arrange.

- *Debrief* When every child has gone, it is worth gathering all the team together to check that everyone is happy, to talk about any problems that have arisen, to encourage each other and pray. Deal with any individual problems separately. Everyone will be tired so this debrief should be *brief* and focused.

Step 7

Enjoy the event, but take time to evaluate it three or four weeks afterwards and start to plan the next one.

Sample Registration Form:

HOLIDAY CLUB REGISTRATION FORM

Name _____

Age _____ Date of birth _____

Address _____

_____

_____

School _____ year_____

Contact telephone number _____

To be collected by _____

Any medical or other problems which may affect the child

_____

_____

Group name _____

How the programme works

Programme for each day

On registration, children go into the appropriate age group: 5-7 (Greens), 8-11 (Reds). In those colour teams, they form small groups. They are also in teams – Jets or Helicopters. Small groups are therefore identified as Green Jets 1, or Green Helicopters 1, Red Jets 1, etc.

The Runway = Worship, etc., all together
Gate 1 = Teaching/Small groups
Gate 2 = Games
Gate 3 = Craft

Timetable

9.45am	Check-in (Registration)
10am	The Runway (Session 1)
10.45-11.15am	Gate 2 – Reds; Gate 3 – Greens
11.15-11.25am	In-flight Refreshments
11.25-11.55am	Gate 1 – Greens; Gate 3 – Reds
11.55am-12.25pm	Gate 1 – Reds; Gate 2 – Greens
12.25pm	The Runway (Session 2)

Runway

This is intended to be a blend of music, fun and inspiration. You may like to divide the area in front of the stage into sections – the Jets on one side and the Helicopters on the other. The children should be sitting on the floor in their small groups with their group leaders, the youngest children at the front for obvious reasons.

The role of the small-group leaders is to encourage the children to listen and learn. They should be themselves, and be enthusiastic. Children learn what to do from their example. They are there to help lead the children in singing and doing any appropriate actions, and help them when they worship. They need to keep alert and watch what God is doing in the lives of their group.

They should not get involved in 'splinter-group' conversations, but direct the attention back to what is happening on the stage. This also includes resisting the temptation to have a little chat with another team member.

NB. Discourage any parents or visitors present from chatting when someone on stage is talking. (They tend to think the 'no-talking' rule does not apply to them, and/or that no one can hear them.)

Team members should exercise any necessary disciplinary control. This does not mean thumping anyone or causing more chaos or disruption! A simple tap on the shoulder and a frown will most often be all that is required.

It is mainly a matter of making sure that no one is fighting or spoiling it for others in any way. It is much better for them to do this than for someone on stage to do a 'headteacher' act! As they get to know their group, the leaders can anticipate any such problems, positioning themselves between persistent 'offenders', for instance.

Children need to be kept back from the stage and away from the overhead projectors, musical instruments and other electronic equipment.

Encourage all team members to feed back any comments/criticisms – they are more able to judge if those on-stage are being effective.

Small groups

These are an essential part of the strategy in the holiday club. The main purpose of the small group is to allow children to know and be known by at least one member of the team. It is a forum to allow the children to talk to you about what they are seeing, hearing, doing, learning and feeling. It is also an opportunity for you to correct any misunderstandings, and for the children to put into practice the things about which they are learning.

Let the group become a 'home group' – a pastoral group that cares for each other and prays for each other. One idea is to have a large piece of plastic sheeting, which each group can make their own (provide suitable pens – make sure the ink stays on the sheet, possibly by writing on the reverse side). This will act as mat (or umbrella) if you are out of doors. It serves as a useful 'boundary' for your group, keeping them together.

The work of the small-group leader may involve teaching, but the holiday club should not be another version of a Sunday school. The intention is that by God's power and grace you encourage the children in your group to become aware of, and respond individually to, what he is doing for each one of them. This is why we emphasise the need for prayer and worship for team members before the day starts.

Registration (Check-in)

Every session begins with registration time. It is important that you have a record of who is with you for each session. If anyone is reported missing it is vital that we know whether or not they actually arrived at our meeting. We suggest the use of a ticket system which, although not 100 per cent foolproof, provides us with physical evidence of a child's presence with us and prevents their leaving at the end of a session without their leader's knowledge. The tickets also contain details of at least one parent's location during that session in case we need to find them in an emergency.

Daily 'tickets'

A sheet of tickets such as those below could be given to each child when they first register. The child hands in the appropriate day's ticket on arrival, and collects it at the end of the day. Each small group should have a register to record attendance.

No child should be allowed to leave without their ticket, which ensures that no child can leave without their leader being aware of it.

Parents could give a contact phone number for emergency use.

A small box could be added which parents could check (✓) to confirm that their child will be picked up at the end of the session – an additional safety measure.

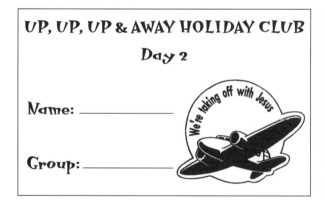

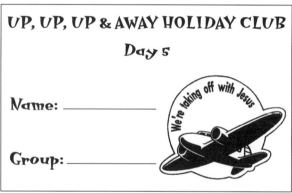

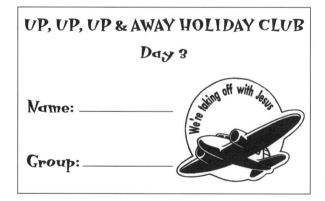

Moving into the worship area

Once you have your group together you can move to THE RUNWAY as the band begins to play. Try to begin on time. Keep any gangways clear, and allow the youngest groups to sit at the front.

Craft and games

The programme also contains specific times for teaching, crafts and games, with a refreshment break at some point. This may mean an amount of movement around the site, so it is important to (a) know where you are scheduled to be, (b) keep your group together, and (c) be kept informed of any changes to the programme, e.g. in the event of wet weather.

During the craft and games sessions you are expected to join in and have a go too! It's important that the children see that you value what they are doing and there is no better way than doing what they are doing. Be sensitive, encourage and help, but don't take over to the point where you exclude the child. Remember, it is when you are doing something together that conversation flows naturally and relationships develop.

Most groups can talk better when engaged in some 'doing' activity. If you wish to take your group away for a walk or a quick game during 'small-group time', please check with your Team Leader before you go off.

Notes about music

Music is a key element in a holiday club. Why? Because music is a kind of 'universal language' that communicates with the heart, and not just the mind. Some wise person once said, 'I don't mind who writes the theology, as long as I can write the hymns!'

There is much evidence to show that adults and children alike learn more theology through what they sing than by any other means. Thus music is not only a means of children having fun, it is also a major teaching tool. From this we should understand that although there is a place for the 'fun song', careful selection of songs is essential in planting biblical facts and principles.

The Runway programme suggests songs for each day of the programme. Some are general praise songs, whilst others are directly connected with the theme of the day. The music for each of these can be found in *Kidsource* 1 and 2 (Kevin Mayhew Ltd). These are not exclusive, and you may prefer alternative songs from other sources that are more suitable for you and your event. For instance, it may be useful to consult your local schools, as they may have some useful suggestions for the repertoire.

Live music

'The best for children, not second-best!' This is a motto worth keeping. Live music is always best, and we suggest you try and find a group of musicians who are willing and available to practise and play the music. These may be adults and/or young people. The main criterion should be 'the best possible'. Drums, keyboard/piano and guitar are a good minimum, but of course there is no set rule, and if you have more musicians, then fine. If possible, in that case, find someone who is able to arrange the music, so that there is quality in the performance. (Not everyone has to play the melody, for instance.) If your church has a CCL music licence (not just the ordinary licence), you will be able to photocopy several copies of the music, and so provide each musician with a folder of the songs to be used.

Recorded music

If there are no musicians available, all is not lost. It is possible to work with recorded music. The music could be played by musicians at a time when they are available and recorded for use at the holiday club. I would suggest using a minidisc for this, as it can used like a CD, with no need to 'rewind' if you want to repeat a song, and the ability to jump straight to the selected track. Minidiscs can be re-used over and over again, and are more versatile and durable than cassettes, though the equipment is a little more expensive initially.

As an alternative, if you know someone with a CD writer as part of a computer, they may transfer your recording from a cassette to a CD, which would mean no special equipment for play-back.

All the suggested songs are available as backing tracks. These are generally the musical arrangements used on the original recordings, but with the voices replaced by a melody instrument. Some albums of children's songs have the backing tracks included on the vocal cassette/CD, sometimes as 'split-track stereo' (which means the voices are recorded on one channel, and by changing the stereo balance of the CD player, you can 'turn the voices off').

Music played by these means is limited by the arrangement used at recording stage. The number of verses, choruses and the key in which it is sung is predetermined.

The other alternative way of providing music is the use of *midi files*. The music is recorded on some kind of computer/synthesiser and played back through a similar device. Many modern keyboards have such a device. It is possible simply to have someone play the songs on such a keyboard and store them on floppy disc (just like a computer). The music can be played back by the keyboard at the holiday club. There are dedicated midi-file players, but these are quite expensive. The great advantage of midi files is that the tempo and key of the music can be changed to suit the occasion. In some cases (depending on the equipment used) the number of verses/choruses etc. can be easily changed, too.

Words

Obviously, the children need to be able to see the words of the songs. Most would generally agree that individual song-sheets or books are inappropriate for this occasion. There are three alternatives.

1. Large song-sheets The words could be written (in lower-case letters, of course) on large sheets of card, in a suitable size to be read by those at the back of the hall. In these days of computer technology and 'copy-shops', it should not be difficult to get these done at reasonable cost. Whilst no projector of any kind is required, there is a need for some way of displaying the cards.

2. Overhead projector The words are written on sheets of clear acetate by hand, or (preferably) printed from a computer. Again, the size of font used should be determined by the ability to read clearly from the back of the hall. Be aware that some overhead projectors need to be placed further away from the screen than others – a factor to be borne in mind when setting out the Runway area.

3. Video/data projector In this case, the words are stored on a computer and thrown on to the screen via the projector. This is the most expensive method, and additionally requires more 'controlled' lighting conditions, unless a powerful model is used.

In all cases, copyright permission is required for the words of songs. If your church has a CCL licence, this is automatically covered.

NB. Good, clear, visible words are important, but so is the leader, for children (especially the younger ones) often tend to lip-read and copy the actions of the leader, rather than read the displayed words.

Actions

After more than 30 years of experience in ministry, I am convinced that appropriate actions or movements are very helpful to most children, as well as being enjoyable. However, not all songs have, or need, such actions. Neither do all children love doing actions. Some books attempt to describe or illustrate such actions. Some recent CDs of children's music (including my own *Ready To Go* and *Keep On Growing* albums) include a CD-ROM track which contains video recordings of the actions for some of the songs – much easier to understand than words or diagrams!

Many adults get embarrassed by actions – and indeed, their children are highly embarrassed if their parents do silly things they never do at home! One important way of assisting in this is the use of signing. Sign language (in particular BSL – British Sign Language) is the third language of this country. It is fairly easy to learn some of the signs for the common words used in worship songs, and to use them where appropriate. Where it is too complex to sign a whole song, I use them just for part of a song, or perhaps use a mixture of signs and simple actions. My main piece of advice, however, is to say that whoever leads such actions must be visible to the congregation, and must be convinced/committed to them. They must be enjoyed, but non-verbal body language (e.g. embarrassment) is contagious, and children will be uncertain as to what they should do.

Training and preparing the team

Introduction

It is important to have some kind of team preparation before the event. Not only does this ensure that everyone knows what they are doing, but it also helps in the process of team-building. This section contains material to help the effective working of the small groups, but we suggest that everyone on the team will benefit.

Leader's notes

Two sessions are planned, each for about 90 minutes.

Summary of Session 1: 'What we are doing and why'
The first session starts by looking at the reasons for holding the holiday club, as discussed in the Introduction. It will examine the values we hold about children, and the principles of small groups and being a small-group leader, a key to the effective holiday club.

Summary of Session 2: 'What we are doing and how'
This session looks at the practicalities of small groups. It will look at each theme to be covered, and the small-group role in the learning process. It is suggested that the craft and games activities are explained for each day.

Session 1

In the 'Practical tips' section, pp. 9–14, we made the following suggestion:

Setting the target Deciding the aim of the event is crucial. Just to run the club is not a particularly good aim in itself. Are you aiming to reach unchurched children? Do you want to build on contacts made in the local school? Do you want to have a special time of encouragement for your regular children? Or are you wanting to offer child minding facilities for the community? Each of these is valid, and your aim may be a combination of two or more of these. Whatever is decided must be accepted by all involved – including the church leadership.

Talk about the decisions that were made about the purpose of your event, so that everyone is clear about the ultimate aims. In the Introduction, the following is stated:

Our aim for children is to give them the dignity of knowing who they are in Christ, and to give them a taste of what God has for them now, not just in the future.

Take time to discuss this aim, and, if necessary, reword it to suit your situation. It may be helpful to go through some of the other points made in the Introduction before the discussion.

Alongside the aims it is helpful to know the values you hold for this work. Values are the building blocks. I have summarised these building blocks as follows:

STATUS as People Children are people, immature, but not inferior.

STATUS as Pilgrims Jesus said, 'The Kingdom of heaven belongs to such as these . . .' (Mark 10:10-13). Wherever they are, our goal is to help move them on in the Christian Journey as fellow-pilgrims with us.

STATUS as Partners As younger partners, they need our protection; our role is to provide the best resources for their growth in faith, to be a pattern to copy (to apprentice children), and to make the whole thing a pleasure!

STATUS with Parents Parents have the prime responsibility for the nurture of their children. Our role is to support them in that responsibility, and to make sure they know what we are offering their children.

These values are important for this type of event as part of children's ministry. Consider the **relationship** children have with God and with you as the team (God's agents).

Consider the **resources** you use – the materials and the team itself. Consider the **relevance** of what you do and teach, that it relates to life as children experience it today, but firmly rooted in God's word.

Make sure it is **really good** – children deserve the best, not second-best!

Discuss these values, as a result of which you may want to add to them.

Small groups

It is a known fact that people of all ages learn more and develop faith quicker as part of a small group or cell. The large congregation (in our case 'The Runway') serves well in inspiration and encouragement in our identity as part of the larger body. However, we grow best when we are able to participate. This is only feasible as part of a small group.

In addition, the small group allows us to develop relationships with others – to be known and accepted and to find our role in relation to a small number of others who are equally seeking to be known and accepted.

A small group may be any number between 3 and 15 – Jesus chose a group of 12 to be with him. In children's ministry, one of the key things in small-group size is the ability for each child to speak and be heard. If there is not much time for such participation, the smaller number is preferable, but there are no clear rules about this. We should remember that there are always some whose verbal contributions are rare.

Keys to an effective small group

1. Clear purpose Know what you wish to achieve. Does the whole group understand and agree to that aim? In a way that is appropriate to the age-group, tell the group what you hope will happen as you get to know each other during the week, and why your group is important. Ask if they are willing to work together to achieve that aim. It is sometimes called 'making a contract'.

The teaching is only part of the agenda, and the groups are more pastoral in nature. We are trying to see where the children are in relation to God, and how meaningful that relationship is to the child. We are seeking to discover if there are problems, hurts or misunderstandings that need a healing touch from our heavenly Father.

2. Building relationships As a small-group leader, invest much of your time in your group. In the first few days, be creative and do things that will help your group to get to know each other and get to know you.

Pray, asking God for a love for each individual. Learn their names and other things about each child, things that are special to them – a hobby, a pet, a favourite toy, etc.

Note: You may not be able to achieve this in the first 24 hours! Ask the Holy Spirit to help you. Use any opportunity to chat with each one outside of 'small-group times'. Make notes afterwards if it will help you to remember.

NB. Try to make sure that you give each of the children in your group a fair share of your attention. Be aware of the quiet ones, but ask the Lord for sensitivity. Avoid doing things which may be seen as 'favouritism'.

Do preserve the dignity of each child and respect things told to you in confidence. If you think an issue needs to be shared or other people should be involved, then you must first ask the child's permission and abide by their wishes in the matter. If you suspect that a child has been abused in some way, please tell your team leader.

3. Preparation Though the groups may be primarily pastoral in nature, it is important to prepare your material, thinking how it may relate to each child in your group. Feel free to adapt it as necessary to meet the needs of the children. However, be careful not to set an agenda that is actually to meet your own needs!

Be aware, too, that many Sunday school teachers do not do well because they are 'task orientated'. They see their purpose as 'doing the lesson'. As we have often said, the purpose of teaching is that children learn, not that we successfully present a lesson. If they do not learn, we are not teaching! This may be because we do not understand the process of learning, of motivating a child to learn, and the need to provide a variety of learning methods (as compared with teaching methods). It may also be that there is no 'anointing' on that teaching – it may not be your gifting.

4. Use the children Groups will consist of a mixture of children. Some will know a lot, some will know little. Some will have been to a Sunday school (or whatever it may be called), for some it will be their first experience. Identify the children who have a fair experience of Bible teaching and get them to share what they know with those who don't know much. We are stretching them, making them a resource, rather than assuming each child is at the same stage of their Christian journey. Equally, there may be those who have had more experience – use that experience – develop their faith and ministry.

5. Discipline The biggest anxiety and cause for distress for small-group leaders is the disruptive child or group. Here are some practical tips to help you:

a) Establish your leadership, helping the children understand that you have the responsibility for the group. There is no need to 'bribe' the children by giving them sweets etc. By all means be kind and generous to them, but be careful not to create problems for other small-group leaders who cannot be so generous!

b) Pray, for Satan will use an unhappy child or an insecure group to bring chaos and discouragement. He wants to rob children of what God would give them. Ask for the gift of discernment, and don't assume there is a demonic cause for disruptive behaviour. Children are far more complex, and there are no easy answers to some needy children.

c) Call in help. Apart from your team leader, there are normally one or two 'floaters' able to take an individual child who is causing trouble for you and the group. To call for help is not failure.

We are not all small-group experts, and we must not judge our performance by comparing our group with another. Each group is different. Actually trust that God has had a hand in teaming you up with your group, and that there is something he wants to do in you and through you.

Generally speaking, as relationships develop, with mutual love and respect, discipline problems diminish. Remember that children are children! It is their nature to be excitable – it is part of their immaturity. It is not unusual for a child to be heavily anointed by the Holy Spirit one moment and fighting with a friend the next!

Remember, too, that the children are on holiday, but they may have had no choice about being here – understandably a reason for resentful behaviour. Love that unruly child, respect him/her and make them feel valued. Minister to them, but be careful again that one child does not dominate and set the agenda for the whole group.

Task

In twos or threes, answer the following: Which of these 'Keys' is most helpful to you? Which gives you most cause for concern? If time permits, share your answers with the whole team.

Touching children

Touch and the display of affection between team members and children is a sensitive issue. This is particularly so in the light of the increased number of reported cases of child abuse (some involving Christians). Some children's evangelists allow no physical contact, not wanting team members to become 'parent-substitutes'. In some family situations, the mother or father may be unable to display affection to the child. A 'rival' affection can arise which may be destructive. We must be careful not to do anything which can be misunderstood by the children or their parents.

Younger children are especially affectionate. We must be careful not to encourage too much affection, yet not give the child any sense of rejection.

The problem of children sitting on your knee etc. is one of trying to avoid favouritism. Each child must feel special, safe and secure. Some will not want physical contact! You may wish to have a special cushion, and only when that is on your lap may a child sit there.

Accidents do happen. On a practical note, picking children up to carry them on your shoulders etc. can result in falls – please be careful. Children are exposed to sexuality and sexual behaviour before they are emotionally or psychologically ready for it, and may innocently do things of a 'sexual' nature without realising the significance. We must not open ourselves to the enemy, who would seek to destroy what we are doing by innuendo and suspicion.

It is our joint responsibility to advise each other if we feel we are going a bit too far or being unwise. This is not 'telling tales' or acting 'holier than thou' – it is acting responsibly, even if we get it wrong. Never go off with a child alone (e.g. for counselling) – keep in sight of others. This is especially important for male team members.

It is a command of Scripture that we love one another – and touch is part of the expression of love. 'Jesus took children in his arms, put his hands on them and blessed them' (Mark 10:16). However, it is wrong for us to use children to meet our need to be loved. That is abuse. On the other hand, we do not feel that we must keep the children at arm's length. Some children need a gentle, reassuring touch. We must be sensitive – holding a hand, or a hand on a shoulder is often sufficient for children to feel your care. Always ask permission.

In view of child protection issues, this section is important. Allow time to discuss any concerns and practical applications in your situation. Make sure everyone has read and signed the team form which contains child protection criteria.

Conclusion

In groups of three, pray for each other, particularly for any personal concerns which may have arisen in discussion.

Session 2

This is a very practical session.

1. The daily programme Give each person a copy of the daily timetable, and make sure they know where they are expected to be at any given time.

2. Toilets and first aid Establish who is the first aider and where they can be found during the day. This person will be responsible for the first aid box. Clarify the procedure for children wanting to use the toilet. Do they need to be accompanied? If so, who takes them, ensuring children are not left unsupervised?

3. Decoration This is an opportunity to plan the overall decoration of the hall/room and also for the small-group leaders to plan the decoration of their 'hangars'. Use the time to share ideas and talents. Some may be particularly able, and it may be an opportunity to bring in others who cannot otherwise be part of the team.

4. Songs It is helpful for the team to learn at least some of the songs and actions before the event.

5. Craft and games The small-group leaders will accompany their children to these activities. It is again helpful for them to have an idea what the children will be doing, because they will be modelling and supervising the children. Allow the craft and games leaders to share an overview of what they plan to do and to demonstrate any particular activities they feel necessary. You may like to give an opportunity for a hands-on session with the actual craft projects, especially any that may require more help.

6. The teaching material *Divide into age groups for this section.* Those not involved in small groups could do any other planning/preparation for the event, or spend the time praying together.

Give each small-group leader (and any helpers, if appropriate) a copy of the small-group teaching notes for their age group. (If possible, give these out before the Training Session – perhaps at the end of Session 1.) Go through the material, ensuring everyone understands the themes and what is expected. Allow time for open sharing of ideas. Encourage every-one to prepare their material well ahead of the event.

Conclusion

Bring everyone together, and spend time praying and worshipping together.

THE RUNWAY

ALL-TOGETHER TIMES OF WORSHIP AND TEACHING

The Runway Songlist

(NB. Some of these are alternatives, so not all may be used)

As I look around me
Building
Can we love one another?
Clap your hands
Good or bad
Here's a song
I am so glad
I'm inright, outright, upright, downright happy
I'm special
In all the galaxy
I will always follow Jesus
Jesus' love has got under our skin
Just as the Father sent you
Keep on going
La la la la la
Life is like a big wide ocean
There is no one else like you
There on a cruel cross
Up, up, up and away (theme song)
We praise God
We're going to praise the Lord
Wherever he rules
Whether you're one

*Of course there may be other songs which are equally appropriate.
The above are only suggestions.*

Day 1: Kingdom love

Bible story

Jesus washes the disciples' feet (John 13:1-17).

Session 1

Songs

We praise God   *or*   We're going to praise the Lord
Whether you're one   *or*   Special

Prayer drill

In the manner of airline cabin crew giving safety instructions:

To the sides *(Point with both hands to each side)*
To the rear *(Point with both hands over the shoulders)*
To the front *(Point with both hands to the front)*
To the Lord *(Lift both hands up, looking up at the same time)*

The *Up, up, up and away* prayer:
Father, thank you for sending Jesus to show your love for us,
and your plan for our lives.
Through the Holy Spirit, help us to 'take off' as we follow Jesus,
and to enjoy the adventure of faith.
In Jesus' name we pray. Amen.

(For the 'Amen', mimic a plane taking off, with a long 'Ah' rising in pitch.)

Song

Up, up, up and away (theme song).

Teaching

Puppets   *or*   The play

In the Governor's country, Frederick Arthur Grasper, owner of FAG (The Fast Airline Group) is not happy about a new arrival to the Governor's country. Vanya, from Banandra, has no valid passport. Grasper forgets the love and acceptance shown to him years earlier, when he and his employee, Boggles, arrived in the country.

Teaching conclusion

Memory verse

Jesus said, 'Here is my command. Love each other, just as I have loved you.' John 15:12 [NIRV]

Songs

Can we love one another?   *or*   Jesus' love has got under our skin
Clap your hands   *or*   As I look around me

Prayer drill

Song

Up, up, up and away

Session 2

Songs
Whether you're one   *or*   Special
Can we love one another?   *or*   Jesus' love has got under our skin
Clap your hands   *or*   As I look around me
(i.e. whatever was chosen for Session 1)

Prayer drill (and prayer)

Song
Up, up, up and away

DON'T FORGET TO USE 'AIR TRAFFIC CONTROL' TO ADD SOME FUN, OR TO HELP RESTORE ORDER, etc.

Teaching notes: All you need is love!

Kingdom love

Love is the keynote of Good News of the Kingdom of God. It is the main characteristic of God revealed in Jesus. Love is a word that is often used carelessly. Our task is to help children realise that God's love for us is real, measureless, and undeserved. The consequence is that we should be those who love others as a 'reflection' of what we have received.

Bible story

Jesus washes his disciples' feet (John 13:3-17)

The play

In the Governor's country, Frederick Arthur Grasper, owner of FAG (The Fast Airline Group) is not happy about a new arrival to the Governor's country. Vanya, from Banandra, has no valid passport. Grasper forgets the love and acceptance shown to him years earlier, when he and his employee, Boggles, arrived in the country.

Teaching outline

Teaching aids A globe or world map; a tape measure, weighing scales, a heavy (though not too large) object and a container of water big enough to hold the object – a bowl to contain the water that overflows, and a jug to measure that water. Picture of Jesus on the cross, or perhaps a crucifix.

When Jesus came, he said he had 'Good News', and he said it was about the Kingdom of God *(show the globe or world map)*. If you were to look for it, you will not find a country called 'the Kingdom of God'. Jesus was saying that wherever people loved and obeyed God, wherever they loved and obeyed King Jesus, that was 'the Kingdom'. He said the Kingdom is inside a person, in the part of us we sometimes call our 'heart' but is not the bit of our body that pumps blood round so we can live! Wherever Jesus is King – that is where we can 'find' the Kingdom. The Kingdom is not just in heaven, when we die, it is also here and now, when we do the things that please Jesus. This week, in our holiday club, we are thinking about some of the 'signs' of the Kingdom, that make it Good News for us and for other people.

Either demonstrate, or get children to volunteer to measure various things – height of another child, weight of an object, volume of an object (by displacing water and measuring water, etc.). The latter can be a bit messy, so prepare well!

Some things are difficult to measure. How can we know how old is a tree? How old is a cat? How clever are you?

How can we measure how much someone loves us?

We use the word 'love' in different ways. When someone says, 'I love ice cream' – are they going to marry the ice cream? It is easy to be deceived – someone may *say* they love you, but their actions may show us differently.

Real love is one of the 'signs' of the Kingdom, perhaps the most important sign. When God says, 'I love you' – it's not just because he *likes* you, and it's not that he says it just to persuade you to do something for him. When God loves us, he just loves us – he will always want the best for us. It's not because we are good enough – he never loves us as a kind of reward for being good. In fact, he will always love us, even if we never show our love for him.

How can we really know that? How can we measure that love? (*Show the various measuring tools you have used.*) The best answer is by looking at Jesus. Jesus never did anything for selfish reasons (make sure the children understand what 'selfish' means). He loved Father God, and he loved people. Everything he did showed us that love. His special friends, the disciples, understood that, even before the day we call Good Friday (*show the picture of the cross or the crucifix*).

When Jesus allowed himself to be taken prisoner, and even to be killed like a criminal – it was all because he loved Father God (and so he did what God wanted him to do) and because he loved us – because it was the only way we could be forgiven and become God's friends. We do not understand *how* that is true, but by *faith* we believe what the Bible says. Real love is costly – it means we put the person we love before our own needs and wants.

The most important thing anyone can do, is to say 'yes' to Jesus, and allow him to love us deep inside, and to let that love heal us and forgive us, and make us the best we can be. Perhaps this week, some of us will say 'yes' to Jesus – even if we've said it before.

Kingdom Love is not just about God loving us – it's about us loving him. The first and great commandment, Jesus said, is to love God with everything we have and are. But the second commandment, he said, is to love others as much as we love ourselves.

How can Jesus measure how much we love him?

FOR THOSE USING THE PLAY

We're going to think about the answer to that question, but before then we're going to use our imagination to visit a small country – the Governor's country, and meet Mr Grasper – Frederick Arthur Grasper (to give his full name), who owns the FAG – the Fast Airline Group, and one of his pilots, Boggles . . .

THE PLAY

[AFTER THE PLAY]
Grasper had forgotten how much the Governor had forgiven him, and was not willing to allow Vanya to enter the country without a passport. Only Boggles remembered how generous the Governor was, and he was going to do the same.

Jesus once went as a guest of a religious teacher, called Simon. (Summarise the story in Luke 7:36-47, emphasizing that what the woman did was a kind of measure of her love for Jesus, because she had been forgiven.) It is easy to *say* we love Jesus, but how can we show it? That is our task today.

Show the memory verse and learn it together.

FOR THOSE USING THE PUPPET PLAY

Jesus once went as a guest of a religious teacher, called Simon. (Summarise the story in Luke 7:36-47, emphasizing that what the woman did was a kind of measure of her love for Jesus, because she had been forgiven.) It is easy to say we love Jesus, but how can we show it?

Jesus wanted his friends to understand how important this was, and on the night before he was killed, he did something extraordinary. Let's watch the story performed by the puppets.

THE FOOT-WASHING PUPPET PLAY

[AFTER THE PUPPETS]
Washing the dusty feet of visitors to somebody's home in that part of the world was the job of the lowest servant, and Jesus was showing that no one is too important to serve others. Jesus did it, and so must we. What can you do to serve others? Let's learn a verse from the Bible – a command from Jesus.

Day 2: Kingdom justice

Bible story
Parable of the unforgiving servant (Matthew 18:23-35)

Session 1

Songs
Up, up, up and away
Wherever he rules   *or*   La la la la la

Prayer drill
In the manner of airline cabin crew giving safety instructions:

To the sides *(Point with both hands to each side)*
To the rear *(Point with both hands over the shoulders)*
To the front *(Point with both hands to the front)*
To the Lord *(Lift both hands up, looking up at the same time)*

The *Up, up, up and away* prayer:
Father, thank you for sending Jesus to show your love for us,
and your plan for our lives.
Through the Holy Spirit, help us to 'take off' as we follow Jesus,
and to enjoy the adventure of faith.
In Jesus' name we pray. Amen.

For the 'Amen', mimic a plane taking off, with a long 'Ah' rising in pitch.

Song
I'm inright, outright, upright, downright happy

Teaching

Puppets   *or*   The play
Vanya, a citizen of Banandra, has arrived in the Governors' country. At first she was refused entry to the country by Frederick Arthur Grasper, owner of the FAST AIRLINE GROUP, who claimed she was unsuitable for the Governor's country and could not have a passport. Boggles, a pilot, was angry at this, and instantly formed BFC – the BOGGLES FLYING COMPANY. This meant that under the laws of the country, he could grant entry to Vanya, and promise her a passport from the Governor, who loves all who come to him and his country. This did not please Grasper, who believed that even the Governor should not simply give a passport to Vanya.

Teaching conclusion

Memory verse
Put up with each other and forgive anyone who does you wrong, just as Christ has forgiven you. Colossians 3:13 [CEV]

Song
I'm special   *or*   There on a cruel cross

Prayer drill

Song
Up, up, up and away

Session 2

Songs

La la la la la   *or*   I'm inright, outright, upright, downright happy
I'm special

Prayer drill (and prayer)

Song

Up, up, up and away

DON'T FORGET TO USE 'AIR TRAFFIC CONTROL' TO ADD SOME FUN, OR TO HELP RESTORE ORDER, etc.

Teaching notes: Forgiveness

Kingdom justice

God is love, but God is just. Yesterday we thought of God's love shown to us in and through Jesus. We don't deserve God's love, yet he gives it freely. It is easy to imply that sin does not matter, because God loves us anyway. Jesus taught of God's forgiveness, and yet he paid the price of that forgiveness. 'There is no such thing as cheap grace,' someone once said.

Our task is to help children take forgiveness seriously – both confessing sin and forgiving it. There are some hard things about forgiveness. If we break a window, we may be forgiven, but we may have to pay for it to be repaired. Jesus Christ paid for our forgiveness as far as God is concerned – but sometimes we must still be punished. Be aware of this as you teach this very big subject, asking God for his help and understanding.

Bible story

Parable of the unforgiving servant (Matthew 18:23-35)

The play

Vanya, a citizen of Banandra, has arrived in the Governors' country. At first she was refused entry to the country by Frederick Arthur Grasper, owner of the FAST AIRLINE GROUP, who claimed she was unsuitable for the Governor's country and could not have a passport. Boggles, a pilot, was angry at this, and instantly formed BFC – the BOGGLES FLYING COMPANY. This meant that under the laws of the country, he could grant entry to Vanya, and promise her a passport from the Governor, who loves all who come to him and his country. This did not please Grasper, who believed that even the Governor should not simply give a passport to Vanya.

Teaching outline

Teaching aids Magic 'washing machine' (see Appendix), two even-sized pieces of cloth, one 'spoilt' with ink (or paint).

Jeremy was excited. He had been invited to the posh house on the big estate. So, after school on the big day, Jeremy rushed home, threw down his school bag and was just about to leave when he heard a voice – 'Jeremy!' It was his mum. 'Wash your hands and face,' said his mum, 'and put a comb through your hair!'

'Oh Mum, do I *have* to?' said Jeremy. He just wanted to go to the big house. Everyone knew that a visit to the house often resulted in a nice present to take home.

'Are you tidy?' his mum asked.

'Yeah, yeah' said Jeremy. As quick as he could, he wiped his face, rubbed his hands on his trousers, gave his hair a quick flick with his mum's hairbrush (he couldn't find a comb) and dashed out of the house.

A few minutes later he was going through the gates of the big estate. It was another few minutes before he reached the door of the big house, where he rang the bell. 'I'm Jeremy,' he said to the lady who stood there.

'I was expecting you,' said the lady, 'but look at your coat, and your shirt.'

Jeremy looked down at his coat – it was very dirty. He'd been messing around with his friends in the school playground and he'd slipped in the mud a bit. And there was that red stain on his shirt – that was spaghetti at lunch-time. He'd tried to wipe it off, but it got worse.

'I'm sorry,' said the lady, 'you can't come in looking like that. Perhaps next time?'

Poor Jeremy – having dirty clothes spoiled his great day. An old Bible word for when we have disobeyed God etc. is 'unclean'. But no amount of washing or soap-powder can clean this 'unclean-ness' – it's something deep inside. Yet we must be 'clean' inside if we are to be right with God. How can we do this?

(Take the spoilt piece of cloth.) This piece of cloth is rather dirty. The best way of cleaning it is to put it in a washing machine *(produce the box)*. We put the cloth inside here *(drop the cloth in),* add the water *(pretend to add water)* and switch it on. *(You could get the children to help, adding appropriate sound effects.)* But when you take out the cloth *(do so)* nothing has changed – what was wrong? *(The answer you want is that you should add washing powder. Repeat the process, adding 'pretend' washing powder.)* Now let's see what has happened to the cloth. *(Bring out the clean piece of cloth – if you want you may 'carelessly' show the apparently empty box.)* The soap powder makes all the difference. But we are not talking about dirt like ink or paint. No washing powder can make us clean deep inside. So, what can do that?

FOR THOSE USING THE PLAY
Before we answer that question, we're going to visit the Governor's country once again to meet Mr Grasper and Boggles . . .

THE PLAY

[AFTER THE PLAY]
Poor Boggles – he also had a problem with a piece of cloth. Grasper had a problem, too, didn't he? He could not accept that the Governor would so easily grant a passport to Vanya. He had forgotten that he, too, was once in the same position.

'Forgive' in sign language used by the deaf is the sign 'to make clean'. Forgiveness is what makes us clean inside, not washing powder. The Lord Jesus shocked people by forgiving sins – 'Only God can do that!' they said – they did not realise that Jesus *was* God – the Son of God. To forgive someone is not just to use the words – just as to say 'sorry' is not always the same as *being* sorry. When the Lord Jesus was killed, in the way they killed bad criminals in those days, the Bible tells us that, though he could have stopped it, Jesus allowed it to happen. 'Through his blood, our sins have been forgiven,' St Paul tells us (Ephesians 1:7). That does not mean that to do wrong doesn't matter. It cost a lot for us to be forgiven. The amazing thing is that all we have to do is be really sorry (the Bible word is 'repent').

But there is more: throughout his life, Jesus taught us to forgive and forgive and forgive. St Peter even asked Jesus 'How often should I forgive?', and Jesus' reply was to the effect that there was no limit. He taught us to pray, 'Forgive us our sins, as we forgive those who sin against us'. It is not easy. It is not easy for a grieving father to forgive the man who killed his child in a car accident. It is not easy to forgive someone who spoils something that took you a long time to do. Forgiving is not easy, but it is what Jesus tells us to do.

That is what we are going to think about today. Before we finish our Runway session, let's pray that prayer Jesus taught his friends and followers to pray. *(Read the Lord's Prayer, using the overhead projector, with or without the Prayer drill.)*

FOR THOSE USING THE PUPPET PLAY
'Forgive' in sign language used by the deaf is the sign 'to make clean'. Forgiveness is what makes us clean inside, not washing powder. The Lord Jesus shocked people by forgiving sins – 'Only God can do that!' they said – they did not realise that Jesus *was* God – the Son of God. To forgive someone is not just to use the words – just as to say 'sorry' is not always the same as *being* sorry. When the Lord Jesus was killed, in the way they killed bad criminals in those days, the Bible tells us that, though he could have stopped it, Jesus allowed it to happen. 'Through his blood, our sins have been forgiven,' St Paul tells us (Ephesians 1:7). That does not mean that to do wrong doesn't matter. It cost a lot for us to be forgiven. The amazing thing is that all we have to do is be really sorry (the Bible word is 'repent').

But there is more: throughout his life, Jesus taught us to forgive and forgive and forgive. St Peter even asked Jesus 'How often should I forgive?', and Jesus' reply was to the effect that there was no limit.

The puppets are going to remind us of a story that Jesus told:

THE UNFORGIVING SERVANT

[AFTER THE PUPPET PLAY]
Jesus was serious about forgiveness. He taught us to pray, 'Forgive us our sins, as we forgive those who sin against us'. It is not easy. It is not easy for a grieving father to forgive the man who killed his child in a car accident. It is not easy to forgive someone who spoils something that took you a long time to do. Forgiving is not easy, but it is what Jesus tells us to do.

That is what we are going to think about today. Before we finish our Runway session, let's pray that prayer Jesus taught his friends and followers to pray. *(Read the Lord's Prayer, using the overhead projector, with or without the Prayer drill.)*

Day 3: Kingdom living

(Use Day 5 programme for shorter event)

Bible story

Parable of the big feast (Luke 14:15-23)

Session 1

Songs

Life is like a big wide ocean
Wherever he rules   *or*   La la la la la

Prayer drill

In the manner of airline cabin crew giving safety instructions:

To the sides *(Point with both hands to each side)*
To the rear *(Point with both hands over the shoulders)*
To the front *(Point with both hands to the front)*
To the Lord *(Lift both hands up, looking up at the same time)*

The *Up, up, up and away* prayer:
Father, thank you for sending Jesus to show your love for us,
and your plan for our lives.
Through the Holy Spirit, help us to 'take off' as we follow Jesus,
and to enjoy the adventure of faith.
In Jesus' name we pray. Amen.

For the 'Amen', mimic a plane taking off, with a long 'Ah' rising in pitch.

Song

Building

Teaching

Puppets   *or*   The play

Much to the annoyance of Frederick Arthur Grasper, owner of the FAST AIRLINE GROUP, who claimed Vanya was unsuitable for the Governor's country, Boggles had enabled her to receive a passport from the Governor. By a mean trick, Grasper tried to persuade Boggles to send Vanya back to her own country. This did not work, however, but Boggles forgave the mischievous Grasper. But in return, he had asked Grasper for just one small favour. Vanya learns she can trust the pilot, who wants to keep her safe and happy.

Teaching conclusion

Memory verse

Jesus said, 'I came so that everyone would have life, and have it fully.'
John 10:10 [NIRV]

Song

I am so glad   *or*   In all the galaxy

Prayer drill

Song

Up, up, up and away

Session 2

Songs
We praise God
Building

Prayer drill (and prayer)

Song
Life is like a big, wide ocean

DON'T FORGET TO USE 'AIR TRAFFIC CONTROL' TO ADD SOME FUN, OR TO HELP RESTORE ORDER, etc.

Teaching notes: A really full life

Kingdom living

Another sign of God's rule is the quality of life we live here. Most people become interested in becoming Christians when they see that we have something they don't – and they want it!

Bible story

Parable of the big feast (Luke 14:15-23)

The play

Much to the annoyance of Frederick Arthur Grasper, owner of the FAST AIRLINE GROUP, who claimed Vanya was unsuitable for the Governor's country, Boggles had enabled her to receive a passport from the Governor. By a mean trick, Grasper tried to persuade Boggles to send Vanya back to her own country. This did not work, however, but Boggles forgave the mischievous Grasper. But in return, he had asked Grasper for just one small favour. Vanya learns she can trust the pilot, who wants to keep her safe and happy.

Teaching outline

Teaching aids A rotten or bad apple; a good apple; an old game, suitable for very young children, wrapped in a parcel; a computer game; a sharp knife; and a cuddly toy.

Sally came in from school one day, and asked her dad, 'Dad, can I have an apple, please?'

'Of course you can,' said her dad. 'Here you are.' *(hold up the bad apple)*

'Thanks, Dad,' said Sally *(with a not-too-happy face)*, 'that's just what I thought you'd give me.'

Rajni's mum came home from work with a parcel under her arm. 'Rajni, you know you wanted that new computer game that all your friends have?'

'Yes, Mum,' said Rajni, a little hopefully.

'Well, I've got you this *(unwrap parcel)* – it's an old game, but I'm sure it will do.'

'Thanks, Mum,' said Rajni, accepting the parcel.

'Look what I've got for the baby to play with,' said Mr Blunt, one day. *(hold up the knife)* 'It's a nice sharp knife – see how it reflects the light – it's very pretty.'

Aren't they silly stories? Surely no real parents would be so horrible and mean to their children? Exactly! Jesus told a similar story one day, ending it with these words: 'Even though you are evil, you know how to give good gifts to your children. How much more will your Father in heaven give good gifts to those who ask him.' (Matthew 7:11)

Sally's dad would have said, 'Look, here's a nice juicy apple.' *(produce the good apple)* Rajni's mum might have said, 'I couldn't afford the really new one, but I asked some of your friends, and they said you'd like this one. *(hold up the computer game)* Perhaps you can use your Christmas gift money to get the other one.'

And Mr Blunt would much rather say, 'Look what I've got for the baby – a nice cuddly toy.' *(hold up toy)*

Today we are thinking about the fact that God wants the best for us. Who has heard of the word 'salvation' or the phrase, 'being saved'? These words mean 'being rescued' and 'becoming the best we can be'.

Some people haven't had a kind and loving dad, and sometimes when they think of our Father in heaven, they might think that God will be just like their dad. But there are other people – boys and girls and grown-ups too, who don't really trust God. They don't believe that God loves us enough to give us what is good for us. *(You may like to do a 'trust' exercise here, inviting someone to come up and fall backwards, saying that you will catch them.)*

Christians are those who have learnt (and are still learning) to trust God – to believe that he always wants the best for us.

This trust is another word for FAITH. To have faith means to believe, or trust, God. This is a gift from God – none of us do it by ourselves. It is God himself who helps us see that what he says in his book, the Bible, is true. It is God who helps us to understand that Jesus really does love us, that he *is* alive and wants to be part of us, and us to be part of him.

FOR THOSE USING THE PLAY
Knowing this is important, for a special reason. But before I tell you why, it's time to visit our friend Boggles . . .

THE PLAY

[AFTER THE PLAY]
Vanya learnt to trust Boggles – that he would not let anything harmful happen to her. Not like Grasper, who seems to be so mean and selfish.

Who would like to be like Grasper? *(Hopefully no hands will go up!)* Of course not, there doesn't seem to be anything nice or attractive about Grasper. Poor old Boggles doesn't seem to be doing so well, though, so perhaps there's nothing especially attractive about him, except he's kind and nice to Vanya.

I said before that it is important for us to know that we can trust Father God. It is important for us to *know* that Jesus really does love us and wants the best for us.

Why is it important? Because, when we live as those who trust Jesus, others will want to know why. Others will want what they see we have. Others need to see that following Jesus doesn't make us miserable – on the contrary – he makes us happy. We are the ones who can tell them and show them that they can have what we have – it's a gift from Jesus.

Sadly, some of your friends will not believe you. Some will not try it for themselves – well perhaps not at first. God will always love them, and will always try to help them see the truth, that he wants the best for us – so that we might be the best we can be.

(Show the memory verse and learn it together)

FOR THOSE USING THE PUPPET PLAY
Jesus said that God's Kingdom is like a man who planned a big dinner – a feast and he wanted *everyone* to come . . .

THE BIG DINNER

[AFTER THE PUPPETS]
Jesus was saying that God's Kingdom is as good as a very big dinner or feast. If his invited guests were going to make excuses, then he'll invite others. The feast is too good to be wasted.

It is important for us to *know* that Jesus really does love us and wants the best for us. Why? Because, when we live as those who trust Jesus, others will want to know why. Others will want what they see we have. Others need to see that following Jesus doesn't make us miserable – on the contrary – he makes us happy. We are the ones who can tell them and show them that they can have what we have – it's a gift from Jesus.

Sadly, some of your friends will not believe you. Some will not try it for themselves – well perhaps not at first. God will always love them, and will always try to help them see the truth, that he wants the best for us – so that we might be the best we can be.

(Show the memory verse and learn it together)

Day 4: Kingdom practice

Bible story
Parable of the sheep and goats (Matthew 25:31-45)

Session 1
Songs
We praise God   or   We're going to praise the Lord
Here's a song

Prayer drill
In the manner of airline cabin crew giving safety instructions:

To the sides *(Point with both hands to each side)*
To the rear *(Point with both hands over the shoulders)*
To the front *(Point with both hands to the front)*
To the Lord *(Lift both hands up, looking up at the same time)*

The *Up, up, up and away* prayer:
Father, thank you for sending Jesus to show your love for us,
and your plan for our lives.
Through the Holy Spirit, help us to 'take off' as we follow Jesus,
and to enjoy the adventure of faith.
In Jesus' name we pray. Amen.
For the 'Amen', mimic a plane taking off, with a long 'Ah' rising in pitch.

Song
I am so glad   or   In all the galaxy *(as Day 3)*

Teaching

Puppets   *or*   The play
Grasper has found out that there is to be a Government Inspection to see which will be the official Airline. The winning Airline will also receive a large sum of money invested in the company. Grasper does not want Boggles to win, and does not tell him about the inspection. What lengths will he go to in order to thwart Boggles?

Teaching conclusion

Memory verse
Jesus said, 'If you love me, you'll obey what I command.'
John 14:15 [NIRV]

Song
I will always follow Jesus   or   I'm enthusiastic

Prayer drill

Song
Up, up, up and away

Session 2

Songs
Here's a song
I will always follow Jesus *(devise a simple folk dance for this)*
or   I'm enthusiastic

Prayer drill (and prayer)

Song
Up, up, up and away

DON'T FORGET TO USE 'AIR TRAFFIC CONTROL' TO ADD SOME FUN, OR TO HELP RESTORE ORDER, etc.

Teaching notes: Make a difference

Kingdom practice

Christians live their lives differently and they do things differently. Yet another sign of the Kingdom is the way we do things – we 'live by the Book', and listen to 'the Word' (Jesus himself).

Bible story

Parable of the sheep and goats (Matthew 25:31-45)

The play

In this episode, Grasper endangers Boggles because he has not followed orders to destroy some dangerous chemicals. Grasper has also found out that there is to be a Government Inspection to see which will be the official Airline. The winning Airline will also receive a large sum of money invested in the company. Grasper does not want Boggles to win, and does not tell him about the inspection. What lengths will he go to in order to thwart Boggles?

Teaching outline

Teaching aids A chair, a bench, a table, eggs, flour, mud, etc. to create an obstacle course; a badly made plastic kit; two different kinds of hat.

Set up a simple obstacle course with eggs, and one or two other messy things. Choose a volunteer and blindfold him or her. The volunteer is to move round the course without touching any of the obstacles by obeying your instructions. *(For fun, when the volunteer is blindfolded, have someone quietly remove the obstacles – don't let the rest of the audience give the game away. Your volunteer can then be guided round an obstacle course that isn't there!)* Do give a small reward if your volunteer really tries to do what he/she is told.

That was just a bit of fun, having to listen to what was said and obeying it. If you have ever seen rally drivers on TV, you will realise what a hard job it is. The navigator is constantly giving instructions to the driver, following instructions on a specially detailed guide – how sharp the next bend is, where to drive on the road, when to brake, when to accelerate, etc. The driver has to listen to each instruction and do it – otherwise the car might crash, or they might lose valuable time.

Many people learn to do a task at first by following instructions. Only when they have learnt what to do, do they not need to refer to the book any more. To ignore the instructions might lead to costly mistakes. *(Produce the badly made plastic kit.)* I didn't follow the instructions for this kit, because I thought I knew what to do, but it has gone a bit wrong – and there are all these bits left over! I can't *undo* it without breaking it, and so it is spoilt.

God wants to teach us things from his special book, the Bible. A Church Army Officer, Captain Tony Maidment, says that BIBLE stands for *Best Instructions Before Leaving Earth*. The instructions are not there just so we can be clever and *know* lots of things – they are instructions on how to have the best in life (as we thought about yesterday).

When God tells us *not* to do something, it is not to spoil our fun, and to make us miserable – it's because he knows what is best for us.

Jesus said something very important for us. He said, 'If you love me, you'll do what I tell you' (John 14:15). Do you remember on Day 1 we thought about Kingdom Love? Jesus said that others would know we follow him not because we go to church, but because we love each other. So what we *do* is very important.

Just as it was not easy for Jesus to do what his Father wanted, Jesus knew it was the best thing, and that God would help him. Like so many of the things we have thought of this week, it is not easy for us to follow Jesus, but remember this: Jesus never asks anything of us that we cannot do. He will always help us if we are trying to do what God wants. Throughout history, Christians have done hard things serving Jesus – the things most other people don't want to do. They do it because it's what Jesus wants, they do it because they love him, and because they love people.

FOR THOSE USING THE PLAY

Before I carry on, we're going to the Governor's country to visit Boggles once again. Grasper knows about some big money for the successful airline, but he's not going to tell Boggles. Grasper gets up to all sorts of shady things – I wonder what he'll do today?

THE PLAY

[AFTER THE PLAY]

Grasper didn't obey the instructions – and something terrible could have happened to Boggles. I don't believe he mistook 'Pest programme' for 'Paste programme'.

But obeying the instructions is important – as we were thinking about before the play. Do you remember the story Jesus told about two house builders? *(put on the 'wise' hat)* Jesus said that one of them took his plans *(take the plan)* and built his house on a foundation of solid rock. *(stamp the 'solid' ground)* It took a lot of work – he had to dig down to the rock first, but he thought it was worth it. The other man *(put on the other hat)* took his plans – maybe even the same plans *(take the plan)* – but when he thought what the other man *(put on the other hat)* had to do – all that digging *(change hats again)* he decided to build his house on easier, softer ground. *(move foot as if kicking the sand)*

But we know what the result of the story is. *(ask the children)* But a more important question is: why did Jesus tell the story? He was talking about the people who heard what he taught, but did nothing about it!

There may be things that Jesus wants you to do, because he knows you love him, and because you try and love others, too. But let's learn those important words of Jesus . . . *(learn the Memory verse)*.

FOR THOSE USING THE PUPPET PLAY

But obeying the instructions is important. Do you remember the story Jesus told about two house builders? *(put on the 'wise' hat)*. Jesus said that one of them took his plans *(take the plan)* and built his house on a foundation of solid rock. *(stamp the 'solid' ground)* It took a lot of work – he had to dig down to the rock first, but he thought it was worth it. The other man *(put on the other hat)* took his plans – maybe even the same plans *(take the plan)* – but when he thought what the other man *(put on the other hat)* had to do – all that digging *(change hats again)* he decided to build his house on easier, softer ground. *(move foot as if kicking the sand)*

But we know what the result of the story is. *(ask the children)* But a more important question is: why did Jesus tell the story? He was talking about the people who heard what he taught, but did nothing about it!

Jesus was really serious about this. He once said that just as a shepherd separates his sheep from the goats, there will be a time when people will be sorted. In heaven he will be looking for people who *do* what he teaches, rather than those who just talk about it.

THE SORTING-TIME PUPPET PLAY

[AFTER THE PUPPET PLAY]

Jesus said that what we do for others is like doing it for him. There may be things that Jesus wants you to do, because he knows you love him, and because you try and love others, too. But let's learn those important words of Jesus . . . *(learn the Memory verse)*.

Day 5: Kingdom choices

(Day 3 for shorter programme)

Bible story
Peter and Cornelius (Acts 10)

Session 1
Songs
Up, up, up and away
Life is like a big wide ocean

Prayer drill
In the manner of airline cabin crew giving safety instructions:
To the sides *(Point with both hands to each side)*
To the rear *(Point with both hands over the shoulders)*
To the front *(Point with both hands to the front)*
To the Lord *(Lift both hands up, looking up at the same time)*

The *Up, up, up and away* prayer:
Father, thank you for sending Jesus to show your love for us,
and your plan for our lives.
Through the Holy Spirit, help us to 'take off' as we follow Jesus,
and to enjoy the adventure of faith.
In Jesus' name we pray. Amen.

For the 'Amen', mimic a plane taking off, with a long 'Ah' rising in pitch.

Song
Building

Teaching

Puppets *or* **The play**
Frederick Grasper, owner of the FAST AIRLINE GROUP is trying his best to get rid of BOGGLES FLYING COMPANY and get Vanya sent back to her own country. Grasper has learned that there is to be a Government Inspection in the airport, and that the winning airline will receive a large sum of money invested in the company. He was forced to tell Boggles about the inspection, but not about the money. Although he thinks that the BOGGLES FLYING COMPANY will fail the inspection, he would like to be sure.

Teaching conclusion

Memory verse
*The Holy Spirit shows what is true,
and will come and guide you into the full truth.*
John 14:15 [NIRV]

Song
Good or bad

Prayer drill

Song
Up, up, up and away

Session 2

Songs
I'm inright, outright, upright, downright happy
Good or bad

Prayer drill (and prayer)

Song
Up, up, up and away

DON'T FORGET TO USE 'AIR TRAFFIC CONTROL' TO ADD SOME FUN, OR TO HELP RESTORE ORDER, etc.

Teaching notes: Eeny, meeny, mino, mo

Kingdom choices

Living as a child of the King is not always easy. Life is not always black and white – sometimes there are grey areas, and we must learn how to make the best choices, risking getting it wrong.

Bible story

Peter and Cornelius (Acts 10)

The play

Frederick Grasper, owner of the FAST AIRLINE GROUP is trying his best to get rid of BOGGLES FLYING COMPANY and get Vanya sent back to her own country. Grasper has learned that there is to be a Government Inspection in the airport, and that the winning airline will receive a large sum of money invested in the company. He was forced to tell Boggles about the inspection, but not about the money. Although he thinks that the BOGGLES FLYING COMPANY will fail the inspection, he would like to be sure.

Teaching outline

Teaching aids Maze, either on OHP acetate, or on a large sheet of card, etc.; silhouette shapes of cloud, head and shoulders of a person, star; picture of a mum and dad; picture of a teacher or some friends; a Bible.

At the beginning of our *Up, Up, Up and Away* holiday club, I said that when Jesus came, he said he had 'Good News' about the Kingdom of God. It is not a place you can find on a map. Rather, Jesus said that wherever people loved and obeyed God, wherever they loved and obeyed Jesus as King, that was 'the Kingdom'. This week, we have been thinking about some of the 'signs' of the Kingdom, that make it good news for us and for other people.

Christians are meant to be different to other people, not because we look different, but because we *are* different – we do things differently, for different reasons, and it is because of our love for Jesus, and our desire to do what he tells us.

Today we are thinking about 'choices' – how do we make the right choices? How do we know if we are right? What help does Jesus give us to make right choices and decisions?

(Produce the maze, with parts of it hidden by the silhouettes) Here is a puzzle – a maze. Let's see if we can do the maze together. *(As you do the maze, help the children see that sometimes they don't know the right way to go, because something is in the way. Only remove the silhouettes once the children have made a choice. This is not meant to be 'heavy'. There is a simple way through which is quite obvious if we could see the whole thing first.)*

It was hard doing the puzzle because of the things that stopped us seeing the way ahead. As we grow up, we may find that life is like this sometimes. Sometimes we have to make decisions or choices. Some choices are easy and obvious. Shall I cross the road now, or wait until there is no danger? Do I want to eat that banana when it is completely black and horrible? Shall I have cat food for tea, or shall I have my favourite meal instead?

Some choices are harder, and depend on what we know, just like doing an exam or test at school. Some choices are hard, because either way seems good (or bad).

FOR THOSE USING THE PLAY

Why do we sometimes choose to do what is wrong? Sometimes we choose to tell a lie, rather than tell the truth. It may be to get us out of trouble, or because we are trying to protect someone. Sometimes we choose to do what pleases our friends, rather than what would please our parents. Sometimes we choose to do what we want, even though we know it is wrong and would hurt Jesus.

How can we make the right choices? What help is there?

Before I answer that question, we're going to visit the Governor's country once more and see what is happening to Boggles . . .

THE PLAY

[AFTER THE PLAY]

Boggles and Vanya had some fun with Grasper, but it looks as if they might miss their chance of passing the Government Inspection. It is very tempting for Boggles to open the case and see what is in it. Vanya asked Boggles, 'What does your heart say? What would the Governor want you to do?'

When it comes to some choices, it is often our conscience which guides us – that something inside us which tells us what is right or wrong.

How do we get a 'conscience'? Well, when we are very young we learn what is right and wrong from our parents. *(show a picture of a mum and dad)* Then when we start school, we learn more from our teachers – and our friends. *(show picture of a teacher or some friends)* When we start to follow Jesus, we learn some things from the Bible. *(show a Bible)*

Which is most important? Well, all of them are important, but we will learn as life goes on that we can trust the Bible, as long as we learn what it really says, rather than just taking some verses.

Some decisions will always be difficult. If we keep close to Jesus, trying to do what pleases him, acting on what we know is true, he will always help us. We need to learn how to hear what he is saying, realising we will sometimes get it wrong. When we get it wrong, we just need to say sorry to Jesus (and mean it) and receive his forgiveness.

Our memory verse today shows us someone else who will help us to make right choices and decisions. Let's learn it together.

FOR THOSE USING THE PUPPET PLAY

Jewish people knew about choices, but they had so many rules and regulations to guide them. Our puppet play today is about Simon Peter making a hard choice. Let's see what it is . . .

PETER AND CORNELIUS

[AFTER THE PUPPET PLAY]

Peter made a right choice – he went into the house of people who weren't Jews, so they also could hear the Good News about Jesus. It was a hard choice – it was against everything he had been brought up to believe. But God helped him.

When it comes to some choices, it is often our conscience which guides us – that something inside us which tells us what is right or wrong.

How do we get a 'conscience'? Well, when we are very young we learn what is right and wrong from our parents. *(show a picture of a mum and dad)* Then when we start school, we learn more from our teachers – and our friends. *(show picture of a teacher or some friends)* When we start to follow Jesus, we learn some things from the Bible. *(show a Bible)*

Which is most important? Well, all of them are important, but we will learn as life goes on that we can trust the Bible, as long as we learn what it really says, rather than just taking some verses.

Some decisions will always be difficult. If we keep close to Jesus, trying to do what pleases him, acting on what we know is true, he will always help us, just as he helped Simon Peter. We need to learn how to hear what he is saying, realising we will sometimes get it wrong. When we get it wrong, we just need to say sorry to Jesus (and mean it) and receive his forgiveness.

Our memory verse today shows us someone else who will help us to make right choices and decisions. Let's learn it together.

Day 6: Family service

Kingdom Attitudes

Bible story
Parable of the sower (Luke 8:4-15)

Session 1

Hymn/Song
e.g. My Jesus, my Saviour

Welcome and introduction

Songs
We praise God   *or*   We're going to praise the Lord
La la la la la

Prayer drill
To the sides *(Point with both hands to each side)*
To the rear *(Point with both hands over the shoulders)*
To the front *(Point with both hands to the front)*
To the Lord *(Lift both hands up, looking up at the same time)*

The *Up, up, up and away* prayer:
Father, thank you for sending Jesus to show your love for us,
and your plan for our lives.
Through the Holy Spirit, help us to 'take off' as we follow Jesus,
and to enjoy the adventure of faith.
In Jesus' name we pray. Amen.

The Lord's Prayer

Song
Up, up, up and away

Reading
Luke 8:4-15 *(Possibly using the Puppet script, unless it is used later)*

Memory verse
Jesus said, 'You must go on growing in me and I will grow in you . . .'
John 15:4 [J. B. Phillips version]   *or*

Jesus said, 'Live in me. Make your home in me, just as I do in you.'
[The Message]

Teaching and introduction to the play

Puppets   *or*   The play
Vanya, the newcomer to the Governor's country, has found a box/briefcase, which they believe belongs to a government observer. They think this box/briefcase contains important information about a special inspection that is due to take place in the airport, an inspection that will decide the fate of the BFC – the BOGGLES FLYING COMPANY. Frederick Grasper, owner of FAG, will do anything to make sure he wins and receives the large sum of money to be invested in the winning company.

Teaching conclusion

Prayer and invitation to respond

Song
I'm special   *or*   Keep on going
We want to see Jesus lifted high

Prayer or blessing

Session 2

Songs
La la la la la   *or*   I'm inright, outright, upright, downright happy
I'm special

Prayer drill (and prayer)

Song
Up, up, up and away

Teaching notes: Mirrors and models

Kingdom attitudes

We keep coming back to the same fact – as Christians we are to be like Jesus. St Paul says of the Holy Spirit, that as we walk close to Jesus, he produces 'fruit' in our lives – characteristics that show we belong to Jesus – not just by what we do, but the kind of people we are.

Bible story

Parable of the sower (Luke 8:4-15)

The play

Vanya, the newcomer to the Governor's country, has found a box/briefcase, which they believe belongs to a government observer. They think this box/briefcase contains important information about a special inspection that is due to take place in the airport, an inspection that will decide the fate of the new BFC – the BOGGLES FLYING COMPANY. Frederick Grasper, owner of the rival airline – FAG – will do anything to make sure he wins and receives the large sum of money to be invested in the winning company. There are surprises in this final episode. The Governor has been watching to see who reflects his nature, and who should be the official airline.

Teaching outline

Teaching aids Large cards with the words Love, Justice, Living, Practice and Choices on them (the Justice card has the word Forgiveness on the back); either some pictures of parents and children, or some actual parents and children (it might be better if they are visitors, and either the children or the parents are not already known by the congregation, for reasons which are explained later).

If you had the shortened programme, you will not, of course, need the 'living' or 'practice' cards. The talk will need to be changed slightly, too.

We have been thinking this week about the Kingdom of God. *(Ask children why we won't find it on a map. Hopefully they will say because it is not so much a place, but it is inside a person.)* That's right. Wherever people loved and obeyed God, wherever they loved and obeyed King Jesus, that was 'the Kingdom'. That's why the Kingdom or reign of God is in individuals – boys, girls and grown-ups. The Kingdom can also be seen in a community, where Kingdom values are not just talked about, but seen in action.

(Hold up card with the word LOVE on it.) We started with LOVE – the summary of God's laws, the motivation for his actions towards us. We learned that Jesus wants us to love others, the way he loves us.

(Hold up the card with the word JUSTICE on it.) We then thought about Kingdom JUSTICE. God loves us, but he is also just. The wrongs we do must be punished, and Jesus took that punishment for us that we might be forgiven. *(Turn card over to show the word FORGIVENESS.)* We

remembered how much Jesus had talked about forgiveness, and how he taught us to be those who did not pay back, but who forgive.

Christians are not meant to be miserable 'kill-joys', Jesus said. *(Ask children to recite the memory verse: 'I came so that everyone would have life, and have it fully.' John 10:10 [NIRV].)* And so our third sign of the Kingdom was *(show the LIVING card)* LIVING. God wants the best for us, and wants us to be the 'best we can be' – another way of understanding the word 'salvation', which is not just about our souls when we die!

'It's not what you do, but the way that you do it', says an old song. Our next sign of God's Kingdom concerned both – *what* we do and *the way* we do it *(show PRACTICE card)*. Many times in the Bible God tells us that it is not enough just to know what he says, we must *do* it, too! If Christians had not *done* what Jesus wanted, the world would be a very different, and a very bad, place.

(Either show the pictures, or the children and parents.) To introduce today's Kingdom value, I wonder if you can guess which child belongs to which parent? *(This is the reason why this would work better if either the parent(s) or the children are not known by the congregation.)*

We linked up the parents with the children mainly because they shared some features. But it is not just the way we look, it is the way we do things that show our parentage – a smile, a cough, the way we walk, etc. It is the same with our heavenly Father. Our final word is *(show the card)* ATTITUDES – *'a state of readiness of a living organism to respond in a characteristic way to a stimulus'.*

St Paul tells us: 'Your attitude should be the same as Christ Jesus' (Philippians 2:5). It is the way we think, the way we respond to life.

FOR THOSE USING THE PLAY:
Before we go on, let us now visit the Governor's country. At the airport, we find Frederick Arthur Grasper, and Captain Boggles, owners of two rival airlines . . . *(Either give the story so far, or let the narrator do it.)*

THE PLAY

[AFTER THE PLAY]
Vanya was not who she appeared to be. As the Governor's assistant, she was looking for the one who had the same attitude as the Governor, and so Boggles was the winner of the inspection.

Kingdom attitudes don't come quickly – they are like fruit growing on a tree. That is why we chose our memory verse for today *(ask who can remember it – and quote it)*. More fruit grow as the tree matures, and as it keeps healthy. So it is with us. St Paul uses the phrase 'fruit of the Holy Spirit' – these are the attitudes that grow in us as we keep close to Jesus, listening to him, worshipping him, doing the things that please him, because we are becoming *like* him.

The purpose of fruit is not just to look pretty, or to give other creatures something to eat. The purpose is to multiply, to reproduce, to spread so that more fruit trees will grow. Jesus wants us to be fruitful – to be like the good soil in the parable. We are the ones God wants to use to spread the Good News of the Kingdom. It is up to us. Are we ready to say 'Yes'?

A PRAYER YOU MAY USE

Heavenly Father, thank you that your Kingdom is Good News. You want the best for us and for all people. Thank you for sending Jesus, so that we could be forgiven and be the best we can be. As we grow in you, and you in us, make us fruitful. We commit ourselves now, as much as we know how, to live our lives for Jesus, so that others may see him in us. We ask for your help in doing the works of the Kingdom, so that the world will be a better place. Come now, Holy Spirit, and give us all that we need to do this. We ask it in Jesus' name. Amen.

FOR THOSE USING THE PUPPET PLAY

Kingdom attitudes don't come quickly – they are like fruit growing on a tree. That is why we chose our memory verse for today *(ask who can remember it – and quote it)*. More fruit grow as the tree matures, and as it keeps healthy. So it is with us. St Paul uses the phrase 'fruit of the Holy Spirit' – these are the attitudes that grow in us as we keep close to Jesus, listening to him, worshipping him, doing the things that please him, because we are becoming *like* him.

Jesus used the picture of 'fruitfulness' often – it was important to him and to us. Our puppets are going to tell us a well-known story of Jesus, perhaps from a different point of view . . .

THE SEED AND THE SOIL

[AFTER THE PUPPET PLAY]

The purpose of fruit is not just to look pretty, or to give other creatures something to eat. The purpose is to multiply, to reproduce, to spread so that more fruit trees will grow. Jesus wants us to be fruitful – to be like the good soil in the parable. We are the ones God wants to use to spread the Good News of the Kingdom. It is up to us. Are we ready to say 'Yes'?

A PRAYER YOU MAY USE

Heavenly Father, thank you that your Kingdom is Good News. You want the best for us and for all people. Thank you for sending Jesus, so that we could be forgiven and be the best we can be. As we grow in you, and you in us, make us fruitful. We commit ourselves now, as much as we know how, to live our lives for Jesus, so that others may see him in us. We ask for your help in doing the works of the Kingdom, so that the world will be a better place. Come now, Holy Spirit, and give us all that we need to do this. We ask it in Jesus' name. Amen.

Memory verses and how to teach them

1. Jesus said, 'Here is my command. Love each other, just as I have loved you.' (John 15:12, NIRV)

2. Put up with each other and forgive anyone who does you wrong, just as Christ has forgiven you. (Colossians 3:13, CEV)

3. Jesus said, 'I came so that everyone would have life, and have it fully.' (John 10:10, NIRV)

4. Jesus said, 'If you love me, you'll obey what I command.' (John 14:15, NIRV)

5. The Holy Spirit shows what is true, and will come and guide you into the full truth. (John 16:13, NIRV)

6. Jesus said, 'You must go on growing in me and I will grow in you . . .' (John 15:4, J. B. Phillips version)   *or*

   Jesus said, 'Live in me. Make your home in me, just as I do in you.' (*The Message*)

Here are some ideas for teaching memory verses:

1. **Jigsaw pieces** Write the memory verse out on card. Cut up into 6-8 jigsaw type pieces. Hide these around the room beforehand. Get the children to find the pieces and put the verse together. You will need a board or something to Blu-Tack the pieces onto as they do this so everyone can see. Then learn the verse.

2. **Hangman** Use an overhead projector or flip-chart. Play hangman to work out the words: you need to put a dash for every letter in every word, spacing the words out. As the children suggest a letter you fill it in every place it comes.

3. **Sorting** This can be a team race if you have two sets of cards. Write the verse out, each word on a separate card. Send the children to collect the cards, and then hold them up at the front whilst the rest of the children decide the correct order. When it is in order learn the verse.

4. **No vowels** Write the verse out but miss out the vowels, using an overhead projector or flip-chart. The children suggest the vowels you need.

5. **Code** Write the verse out in code, either every alternate letter is the one you want so you have to cross out the other letters. Write each word backwards. Write each word with an extra letter at the beginning and end. Again use an overhead projector or flip-chart.

7. **Message board** If funds allow, an electronic message board may be used to display, add (or remove) words from the text.

8. **Balloons** Insert individual words from the text into deflated balloons. Inflate the balloons and position them, either in a bunch or around the room. Children take turns to burst a balloon (you could make a game of this). Sort out the words into the completed text. (For variety, some balloons could have blank pieces of paper.)

GATE 1

SMALL-GROUP TEACHING

Day 1: All you need is love

Theme: Kingdom love

Key verse

John 15:12 – 'Here is my command: love each other just as I have loved you.'

Introduction for leaders

This is our first flight into the Kingdom. We are looking at Kingdom love. We are thinking about how God's love is different to the conditional love we often encounter in the world. His love is constant, perfect, forgiving and unconditional. It is a sacrificial love which we never have to earn, he gives it however we behave. He wants us to love each other in the same way that he loves us. The story today is Jesus washing the disciples' feet (John 13:1-17). Kingdom love starts with God's love for us. It is the first session so it would be helpful to check that the children know that God loves them. Kingdom love continues through our love for others.

The focal point of the story is Jesus showing his love for the disciples by washing their feet, a task normally done by servants. He then exhorts the disciples to copy his example, to serve each other thereby demonstrating love. How do we show love to each other? Does your church family show love? Would other people know that you love each other?

Key teaching focus

To know that in the kingdom we know that Jesus loves us and because he loves us we love each other.

Targets

1. To get to know the children and for them to get to know you.

2. To remind the children that Jesus loves each of us.

3. To think about how we can love each other as Jesus loves us.

Teaching plan for Greens (5-7)

All you need Bowl of water, soap, towel; A4 paper for each child, scissors, pencils or felt tips.

1. Be relaxed and flexible. You should have about 25-30 minutes for this time. Get to know the group and don't worry if you can't fit in all the ideas. You may like to play a name game. Find out a bit about the children, e.g what schools they go to, where they live, how they came – by car, bus or on foot?

2. How do we know who loves us? Ask the children to think about someone they know who loves them (e.g Mum, Dad, carer, grand-parent, friend, brother or sister) but not to tell, to keep it a secret. Then ask them to think of one way that person shows they love them, still keeping quiet. When they have thought of something they take turns to mime the action whilst the others guess what it is and who might be the person doing it.

3. Say that we know people love us because they show it. Tell the story of the foot-washing from John 13. You could illustrate this by washing a child's feet or a leader's. Emphasise that Jesus showed his love for the disciples by washing their feet, by acting as the servant; he also wants us to love and serve each other. Love is actions not just words. Talk about how we can show love to others, and go round the group asking each child to suggest a way.

4. Pray together based on what the children have said. 'Thank you, Lord, that you love us. Help us to love each other, to be kind, and to do things for each other such as . . . Thank you that you have promised to help us through your Holy Spirit. Amen.'

5. Foot cut-outs . . . give each child an A4 piece of paper and pencil. They draw round their foot, cut it out, write their name on and then decorate it with felt tips or crayons. You can use these to decorate your hangar.

6. Worksheet on this teaching which you can use now or send home.

7. Extra – jigsaw puzzle: if time permits you could revise the memory verse, write it out on card, cut up the card into several irregular sections. Ask the group to see how fast they can put it together.

Teaching plan for Reds (8-11)

All you need A4 paper, piece for each child, pencils, large A2 paper, marker pen, string.

1. Be relaxed and flexible. You should have about 25-30 minutes for this time. Get to know the group and don't worry if you can't fit in all the ideas. You may like to play a name game. Find out a bit about the children, e.g what schools they go to, where they live, how they came – by car, bus or on foot?

2. Brainstorm together how we know someone loves us: i.e. by what they do for us. Get someone to write down the ideas on a big sheet of paper. Together read the Bible passage, John 15:12-15. One of the children may like to read it.

3. Tell the story from John 13 of the foot-washing. Illustrate it by washing either a child's feet or a leader's (ask for a volunteer). Emphasise that Jesus showed his love for the disciples by washing their feet, by acting as the servant; he also wants us to love and serve each other. Love is actions not just words. You could play a miming game – the children could take turns to mime a way of showing love for the others to guess.

4. Talk about what Jesus did to show his love for people (spent time with them, prayed for them, healed them). Could we do some of these things today? Some we can, e.g comfort those who are sad or lonely; some may be a bit odd in today's culture, like washing feet; some may take courage and faith, e.g feeding 5000 or praying for friends who are sick. But Jesus said we would do greater things than he did through the power of the Holy Spirit.

5. Give everyone in the group a piece of paper (A4). Ask them to write their name on it then draw something which they enjoy doing, e.g football, riding, playing with a pet. Remind the children that Jesus commands us to show his love in everything we do. When finished string all the pictures together, tie a knot, the circle represents the group where everyone is included and loved and special to God.

6. Pray together asking God to be close to the children and to help the group to be loving to each other, and for us all to know that we are special to God. Do ask whether one or more of the children would like to pray.

7. Worksheet on this teaching which you can use now or send home.

8. Extra: jigsaw puzzle – if time permits you could revise the memory verse, write it out on card, cut up the card into several irregular sections. Ask the group to see how fast they can put it together; use a watch with a second hand to time it.

Day 2: Forgiveness

Theme: Kingdom justice

Key verse

Colossians 3:13 – 'Put up with each other and forgive anyone who does you wrong, just as Christ has forgiven you.'

Introduction for leaders

Our second flight into the Kingdom is about Kingdom justice. First we have to understand that God is holy, fair and just and that our sin separated us from God. *But* God loves us so he sent Jesus to die in our place, to be punished instead of us so now we can be forgiven and become children of God. The other side to Kingdom justice is that because we are forgiven we should forgive other people. The story today is the parable of forgiveness from Matthew 18:21-35. Forgiveness is a difficult word although the concept of being forgiven we understand. Most of us experience doing wrong and knowing 'forgiveness' from parents or friends or teachers. However, the term forgiveness is not commonly used outside the church. It might be helpful to explain it using an example, e.g you play with a friend's toy and break it; you don't know what they will say but you explain and say sorry. They say, 'It's OK. I forgive you.' Sometimes things people do hurt us but we still forgive and don't hold grudges.

Key teaching focus
To know that in the Kingdom we forgive each other as God forgives us.

Targets
1. To understand what sin is and to know that Jesus died that we might be forgiven.
2. To think about what it means to forgive.

Teaching plan for Greens (5-7)

All you need Objects in bag for grab game, big paper, marker pen, scissors.

1. Grab game: Have lots of different objects in a bag, enough for each child; these could include: small wrapped sweet, pencil, safety clip, empty wrapper, Mars Bar, rubber, balloon, and a £1 coin concealed in a piece of Blu-Tack. Tip them out and tell the group to grab something and they can keep what they grab. When done talk about how they decided, what went first; was it fair? who has the Blu-Tack? Make the point that we often decide by outward appearances but God knows what we are like inside.

2. What are we like on the inside? Talk about things we do that are wrong; explain the Bible calls this sin. On the big paper write GOD on one side, US on the other and draw a big chasm in between. As the children suggest 'sins' write them in the chasm. Then draw a cross that reaches between God and Us. Explain that when Jesus died on the cross he dealt with our sin and we can be forgiven for all our wrongdoing and come back to God. Cut out all the sin words to illustrate the point.

3. Story: What does it mean to be forgiven and to forgive? Tell the story from Matthew 18. You could use stick puppets as props, a wooden spoon with a face drawn on and material for clothes. Talk about the story: who is forgiven, who represents God, who represents us, what does forgiveness mean? Think about times when we have felt hurt by others or have hurt others.

4. Prayer time: Use this time to thank God for sending Jesus and for forgiving us, and ask him to help us to forgive other people.

5. Sorry cards: Cut out some card beforehand into aeroplane shapes and write 'I am sorry' on it. Each child has a card and draws/writes on it something they want to say sorry for. They can then colour it.

6. Worksheet for now or to take home.

Teaching plan for Reds (8-11)

All you need A5 paper, pens or pencils, objects and bag for grab game, bin.

1. Grab game: This would be appropriate for this age also. See teaching plan for Greens.

2. What are we like on the inside? We all do wrong which the Bible calls sin. Give each child a piece of paper and a pencil. Ask them to write on it something they would call wrong; then ask the children to read what they have written. Have spare papers for more ideas and make sure that you include things such as lying or kicking your brother, things we do wrong every day. Then lay the papers side by side to form a barrier. Use this to illustrate that our sins form a barrier between us and God but when Jesus died for us he dealt with our sins; he was punished for us. So now when we say sorry to God we are forgiven and all our sins are taken away. Now we can be close to God and be his friend. Remove the paper barrier and rip up all the sins into small pieces and throw into the bin.

3. Story: What does it mean to be forgiven and to forgive? Use the story from Matthew 18:21-35. Tell the story or ask one member of your group to read it from the Bible. Ask the group what happens in the story and discuss who is forgiven; who represents God; who represents us; what does it mean to be forgiven? should we forgive others? Think about times when we have hurt others and when we have been hurt by others. Encourage the group to be honest – and be open yourself.

4. Memory verse: See if the group can remember the memory verse from Runway 1. Read Luke 23:26-43. Tell the children to stand up when you get to the memory verse.

5. Pray together as appropriate following your discussion, thanking Jesus for dying for us and forgiving us and asking him to help us forgive others.

6. Worksheet for now or to take home.

Day 3: A really full life

Theme: Kingdom living

Key verse

John 10:10 – Jesus said: 'I came that everyone would have life and have it fully.'

Introduction for leaders

Our third flight into the Kingdom is Kingdom living. God wants us to live life to the full and that means knowing God and having a relationship with him. Part of God's plan is that we enjoy his world and get the very best out of the life he blesses us with. This does not necessarily mean we get what we want but God has our best interests at heart. God is for us. The story today is the parable of the banquet (Luke 14:15-23). Jesus wants us to celebrate with him. In this session we want the children to grasp that we can really enjoy life in the Kingdom – so often people think that the Christian life is about 'thou shalt nots'. Jesus said he came to give us abundant life. There are two dimensions to this: firstly in everyday life enjoying the things we do and have and the world around us; secondly in spiritual life, the sense of knowing God's love, peace and joy and experiencing his presence and power through the Holy Spirit, and also the hope of eternal life. So Jesus invites us to his feast. Have we accepted or are we still on the outside? Are we experiencing the fullness of life Jesus offers?

Key teaching focus

To understand that Jesus offers us life in all its fullness and that he wants the best for us.

Targets

1. To think about enjoying everyday life.
2. To know that Jesus offers us abundant life and invites us to his feast.
3. To know that Jesus wants the best for us.

Teaching plan for Greens (5-7)

All you need Blank party invitations (one for each child), pencils, felt tips, 16 shopping items for the memory verse, balloons for each child, simple fun food, party game.

1. Miming game: The children take turns to mime something they really enjoy doing, the others have to guess what it is and if they enjoy that also, to join in the mime. TIP: start off sitting in a circle with the mime 'artist' in the middle. Talk about how Jesus wants us to enjoy life.

2. Memory verse: Have 16 items of shopping of differing value, e.g. cereal, choc bar (empty packets would be fine), pens, ball. Put a price label on each item. On each item write one word from the memory verse including the reference but put these on in order of

value (lowest to highest). Get the group to arrange the items in the right order of value then to read the memory verse. Do this several times until they know the verse.

3. Story: Give each child an invitation to fill in their own names. Tell the story from Luke 14, getting the group to act it out as you tell it. Emphasise the fact that Jesus invites all of us but that not everyone accepts. We need to be sure that we have accepted his invitation.

4. Pray together thanking God for all the good things he gives us; encourage the children to suggest things to say thank you for and to take part in the prayer.

5. Jesus wants the best for us: Talk about all God's blessings which includes enjoying everyday life and knowing his Spiritual blessings. Then come to the feast and party. Give each child a balloon to blow up (with help if needed) and then to decorate with felt tips. You may like to share appropriate food such as sweets or biscuits; you may like to have a party game such as 'pass the parcel'. The balloons could decorate your hangar afterwards.

6. Worksheet for now or to take home.

Teaching plans for Reds (8-11)

All you need 16 items of shopping, party game, fun food, pop music.

1. I enjoy: Go round the children asking what they enjoy doing and why. You could make a game of this by asking the children who like similar things to get into a group and see which is the biggest group. Talk about how Jesus wants us to enjoy life.

2. Memory verse: Use the game from Greens (Teaching plan no. 2) but don't put the price on the items. See if the group can guess the order, and see what different versions of the verse you get until they get it right.

3. Story: Ask one of the group to read the story from Luke 14. Discuss how Jesus invites all of us but not everyone accepts. What were the excuses given in the story? Divide the children into three small groups, ask each group to think of a modern-day excuse which they then act out for the others to guess. Emphasise that we need to be sure that we have accepted Jesus' invitation ourselves.

4. Jesus wants the best for us. Talk about all God's blessings including enjoying everyday life and knowing his spiritual blessings. Then pray together; encourage the children to pray aloud thanking God for something he has given us.

5. Party time: you may like to have a party game or pop music to dance to, and maybe have some fun food to share.

6. Worksheet for now or to take home.

Day 4: Make a difference

Theme: Kingdom practice

Key verse

John14:15 – Jesus said: 'If you love me you obey what I command.'

Introduction for leaders

This is our fourth flight into the Kingdom. The teaching is based on Matthew 25:34-46. The focus is not about being judged for what we don't do but about what God wants us to do. The children will be able to understand all these things, being hungry, thirsty, needing clothes, being sick, being in prison even if it is not directly part of their own experience. Love is practical; today we look at what we can do to show God's love. We are learning that what we say we believe must be backed up by what we do. Our aim is to be more like Jesus and to get better at doing things for him. But we can't do this by ourselves; we need the Holy Spirit to help us.

Key teaching focus

In the Kingdom we show that we are following Jesus by what we do, we share God's love by loving actions.

Targets

1. To know that what we do is as important as what we say.
2. To think through what it means to obey the command to love each other.
3. To work out practical ways of showing love to each other.
4. To understand that the Holy Spirit will help us.

Teaching plan for Greens (5-7)

1. 'Simon says' game: You give instructions such as stand still, hop, lie down, jump, hands on head. You preface each command with 'Simon says' but every so often you leave out that preface. The children only do the instruction which Simon says. The children either sit out if they get it wrong, or stay in but get teased for getting it wrong. Ask the children what Jesus commanded us to do.

2. How do we know someone loves us? Talk about who loves us and how we know they do.

3. Jigsaw game: Make a simple jigsaw beforehand by gluing a suitable picture to card, e.g an old magazine picture. Cut up the picture into pieces, matching the number of pieces to the number of children. Give each child a piece and then ask the group to make the picture. Make the point that you need everyone's help to make the picture. You could hide the pieces for the children to find if you have appropriate space.

4. Memory verse – jigsaw link: This activity could be extended by writing the words from the memory verse and reference on ten of the pieces,

a word per piece. The children have then also to read the memory verse when they have completed the jigsaw.

5. Story: Retell the Bible verses from Matthew 25:31-40 or read it from a simple version such as CEV. Talk about what it means. Have they been hungry, thirsty? Needed clothes? Have they ever been ill and needed looking after? Have they ever gone to a new place or school and felt lonely, not knowing anyone? What would it be like to be in jail? Jesus says when we help other people it is as if we are doing it for Jesus, that makes it special!

6. Activity – charades: How can we practically show love to others? Brainstorm together how we can help at home, school, with friends. Make a list of ideas. Divide the group into two, each half works out a scenario in which someone needs help. They act this to the other half who work out what is happening and suggest how that person could be helped.

7. Circle prayer: It is important to emphasise that Jesus has promised that he will help us to be loving through the power of his Spirit. Pray for each other by holding hands in a circle and then asking Jesus to help us be more loving through his Holy Spirit.

8. Worksheet for now or later.

Teaching plan for Reds (8-11)

All you need Objects to make obstacle course, e.g chairs, table, cushions; cards for miming game, pencil, felt tips; A4 card in light colours to make get-well cards either with felt tips or using tissue paper and glue to make collage designs.

1. Obstacle challenge: Set up a simple obstacle course in your area using chairs, cushions, tables, etc. Challenge the children to do this course blindfold. Select one child, put on blindfold and tell the child what to do, e.g. 4 paces forward, bend low, etc. The child then does the course by obeying your instructions. Link this to the memory verse. The child could do the course because he/she obeyed. Jesus has asked us to obey him and to love each other. If you have time others could do the course with the other children giving instructions.

2. Miming game: Divide the group into pairs. Write out on cards the following: being hungry, being thirsty, needing clothes, being a stranger, being ill and being in prison. Give each pair a card and ask them to mime what is on the card for the others to guess. If your group is large you may need to duplicate the cards.

3. Bible reading: Ask one of the children to read Matthew 25:31-46 for everyone. Link this to the miming game. Talk about what it feels like to be hungry, thirsty, etc. Who has been ill? what about being in prison? what is Jesus telling us to do? Concentrate on the doing part but be prepared for questions about judgement. Emphasise that Jesus says that when we help other people in need it is like helping Jesus himself. Wow! Discuss: if we say we follow Jesus we should be loving towards others.

4. Brainstorm: How can we help others? Make this very practical – what can we do to show love at home, school, work, with friends? Give the children a pencil and paper and suggest they write down the ideas.

5. Pray: Remind the group that Jesus promised that the Holy Spirit would help us to be more like him and to be loving, so you are going to ask the Holy Spirit to help us. Either do this all together with the group holding hands or put the children in pairs and tell them to pray for each other.

6. Worksheet for now or later.

7. Get-well cards: You may like to make get-well cards to send to people you know who are unwell, either in the community or known to your group. If you have run out of time this could be a challenge to be done at home.

Day 5: Eeny, meeny, miny, mo

Theme: Kingdom choices

Key verse

John 16:13 – 'The Holy Spirit shows what is true and will come and guide you into full truth.'

Introduction for leaders

Our fifth flight into the Kingdom is about choices. Every day we make decisions and some will be good and some won't, some will be big choices and some will be small. God is involved in every part of our lives; he wants the best for us and he will help us to make the best choices. He has promised that his Holy Spirit will guide us. Sometimes he asks us to do things which we find hard. We have to choose whether we obey, whether we are loving, whether we do right or wrong. In the Kingdom we choose God's way even if it is difficult. The story is about Peter having a difficult choice to make (Acts 10).

Key teaching focus

In the Kingdom the Holy Spirit will help us choose to obey and do what is right and true.

Targets

1. To think about choices we make every day.

2. To know that sometimes it is hard to make the right choice.

3. To know that the Holy Spirit will help us to choose God's way.

Teaching plan for Greens (5-7)

All you need 4 boxes, red, blue, yellow, green; Smarties, toy, 5p coin, straw, white tea towel or sheet of paper, pencils, small pieces of paper, hand puppet (animal or person).

1. Boxes: Have 4 boxes coloured red, green, blue, yellow. Beforehand put some Smarties in the first, a small toy in the second, a 5p coin or similar in the third, and some straw in the fourth. Tell the children what you have put in the boxes but don't say which box. Select 4 children to come and choose a box each without touching it. They then open the box and keep what is inside. Talk about why they chose their particular box. Link it to all of us having choices to make each day. Talk about choosing clothes, ask what they ate for breakfast, what programmes do they watch and why?

2. Story: Have a sheet of white paper or small cloth. Give each child a piece of paper and a pencil and ask them to draw any animal or bird they can think of. Ask the children their favourite food. Retell Acts 10, pointing out that Peter was probably hungry and thinking of his favourite food. Use your sheet and the children's drawings as a visual aid. Emphasise that Peter had to choose whether to obey what God was telling him through this dream.

3. Choices: Tell the children that this week we have learnt about being part of God's Kingdom. We have many choices to make, the first choice is whether we want to be part of the Kingdom and follow Jesus. Then we have to choose whether to obey Jesus and be loving and do the best we can. Use a puppet and tell the group that the puppet can't decide what to do; could they help? Here are some suggestions of choices the puppet has to make: I know Jesus loves me but I don't know if I want to follow Jesus.

   I want to go and play but I promised my mum I would tidy my room.

   I want to watch telly but my grandma is poorly and Mum wants me to go and see her.

   Dad told me not to buy chewing gum but I really like it and I have enough pocket money to buy it.

   I want to play football but there is a new boy/girl who is crying and all by themselves in the playground; should I play with them?

   I like going to the church on Sunday but I like sleeping in as well; what should I do?

   Go through these suggestions one by one on your own, getting the puppet to say them in some way perhaps to you and then ask the children for their ideas.

4. Pray: If you can, pray for each child individually. Ask them what they would like you to pray for. Do give the children the opportunity to say Yes to Jesus and to ask him into their lives as their friend and Saviour. You may also like to ask the Holy Spirit to fill the children so that they can live for Jesus day by day. It would be a good time to invite them to the family service and to talk about any possible regular activity the children can come to either on a Sunday or midweek.

5 Worksheet as usual.

Teaching plan for Reds (8-11)

All you need Big sheets paper, pens, white cloth, cards for choices, pencils, bag or basket.

1. Fire: Imagine there is a fire in your house and you have to leave at once. You can take one thing with you, what would you take and why? Discuss with the children how and why they would choose that object.

2. Every day: Make a list together of the choices that the group has made that morning, e.g. what to wear, what to eat, how to come, whether to watch TV, etc. Emphasise that we have choices to make daily, some are hard if you are following God's way. Ask the children for suggestions. Ask the children their favourite food. Link to the story, saying that Peter had a dream about food.

3. Story: Retell the story of Acts 10. Get one of the children to lie down to be Peter, and as he sleeps get all the others to choose an animal or bird or reptile and to make the noise of that creature when you wave a white cloth over his head. Some of the children could mime being the group sent by Cornelius and Cornelius himself. Ask the

children what the choice was that Peter had; you may need to explain how Peter would have been brought up eating only certain foods.

4. Choices: Explain that sometimes we have to make difficult choices if we want to obey Jesus. Write out on separate cards the following scenarios and put them in a bag or basket and let the group take turns to pick one out, read it and say what they would do. Let he group talk about each scenario.

   I want to go and play outside but I promised my mum I would tidy my room.

   I want to watch telly but my grandma is poorly and Mum wants me to go and see her.

   Dad told me not to buy chewing gum but I really like it and I have enough pocket money to buy it.

   I want to play football but there is a new boy/girl who is crying and all by themselves in the playground, should I do anything about it?

   I like going to the church on Sunday but I don't want to get up, what should I do?

   My friend steals chocolate bars from our local shop; they say it's easy and they will show me how; what should I do?

   When I grow up I would like to be a nurse but I could make more money as a pop star, what should I do?

   My next-door neighbour is very old; she asks me to post a letter for her but I am very busy, so should I go and see her?

5. Pray: If you can, pray for each child individually. Ask them what they would like you to pray for. Do give the children the opportunity to say Yes to Jesus and to ask him into their lives as their friend and Saviour. You may also like to ask the Holy Spirit to fill the children so that they can live for Jesus day by day. It would be a good time to invite them to the family service and to talk about any possible regular activity the children can come to either on a Sunday or midweek.

6. Worksheets as usual.

GATE 2

GAMES SESSIONS

Games sessions

The children enjoy playing games. It is an opportunity to use up some energy. It gives more time to get to know the children and to talk informally, also to model Christian behaviour. There is a session of games each day. I am suggesting six themes for games, one for each day. You can do them in any order or do your own games which you know work well for your group of children. I am making a few suggestions for each theme. There are many more possibilities and some very good books on games you could refer to. I will indicate if the games are more suitable for one particular age group.

Theme 1: Parachute games

Parachute games are fun and also teach the children to work together. You may be able to borrow/hire a parachute from your diocesan office or resource centre.

1. **Revolving** Everyone holds on to the edge of the parachute with one hand, facing the same way. Run round as fast as possible, change hands and go back the other way.

2. **Popping balls** Everyone moves the chute up and down together. Throw on several small light-weight balls and see how high they can go by moving the chute.

3. **'Football'** Everyone holds on to the edge of the parachute with both hands. Children on one half of the parachute play against the other. Use a 'football', each team trying to make the ball go off the parachute on the other team's side. You score if the ball touches the floor. *No touching the ball, you can only move the parachute.*

4. **Swapping** Everyone moves the chute up and down as high as possible, when it is up, call out a category (e.g. anyone 5 years old). The children who are in that category swop places by running under the parachute before it comes down again. Categories could be: ages, wearing different colours, having different pets, wearing different sorts of shoes, going to different schools, watching different TV programmes, what you ate for breakfast, etc.

5. **Cat and mouse** Everyone holds the chute down low. One child crawls around under the parachute (the mouse), another takes off their shoes and prowls around on top of chute (the cat). When you say GO everyone keeps the parachute moving to attempt to hide the 'mouse'. The 'cat' tries to catch the mouse by touching the mouse through the parachute. Repeat until everyone has had a turn.

Theme 2: Team games

1. **Over and under** Divide the children into equal teams. The teams line up. Each team has a ball or balloon. When you say GO the child at the front passes the ball between their feet to next person, and so

on, down the line. The last child runs to the front and starts the process again. The team sit down when the first child comes to the front again. Repeat the game, but send the ball over their heads. The Red groups would be able to do this in alternating fashion, i.e. first child passes the ball overhead, next child between their feet and so on.

2. A variation of the above would be to use balloons: the first team member blows it up then sends it over or under, each team member running to the front to start the process again. When it gets back to the first person they have to pop the balloon, the first team to pop the balloon is the winner.

3. **Balloon volley ball** Divide into two teams. The teams sit opposite each other, with feet touching those of their opposite number. *They must keep their bottoms on the floor at all times.* The team scores if they can get the balloon to touch down behind their opposite team. To start, count to 3 then throw the balloon into the middle of the teams. The balloon must not be held, but kept moving.

4. **Indoor hockey** (Reds) The teams sit opposite each other with about 2m between them. Number off down the line. In the middle you need two 'Uni-hock' sticks and a ball, or rolled up newspaper and a soft ball, or a sock tied into a ball. A chair at each end may act as the goal. Establish who is shooting which way. Call a number and those two children have to get the stick and try to score by getting the ball right through their chair/goal. Call another number after a certain time or after a goal.

5. **Mat ball** (Reds) Divide into two teams. Each team chooses a goalie who stands on a mat or in a hoop at each end. You score when the goalie has caught the ball, but every team member has to have handled the ball before you score. *No running with the ball.* You need a football-sized ball.

6. **Basket balloon** (Reds) Divide into two teams. Each team has a goalie who stands at opposite ends on a chair with a basket or cardboard box big enough to hold a balloon. The teams score when their goalie has caught the balloon in the basket. *The balloon cannot be held, it must keep moving.*

7. **Dribble hockey** Divide into teams (more than two are possible) The teams line up facing a chair. The first child dribbles a ball with a hockey stick down the hall, round a chair and back. They pass the stick and ball to the next child who then goes and so on. When the last child is back the team sits down.

8. **Flat fish** Divide into teams, line up. Each team needs a fish shape cut out of strong paper or card, and a magazine or newspaper. The first child has to wave the paper to waft the fish down to a given point, e.g. a chair, and back to their team. The next child then does the same and so on until all have had a turn.

9. **Team roll** Each team lies down side by side. At a given signal the first team member rolls over the backs of the team until they reach the other side, then the next team member goes and so on until

everyone has rolled over the team. (Safety note: the children should remove shoes before doing this and should be told to keep their heads down. The teams should consist of children of the same size/age.)

10. **Outdoor** type team games suitable for Reds:

   1. *Rounders* You need four stumps for bases. Rounders bat and ball, use a tennis ball if the children are new to this game.

   2. *Shinty* This is a form of hockey, any number per team, using simple hockey sticks and a soft ball. Set up goals with stumps or cones.

   3. *Crocker or non-stop cricket* You need a light football, a rounders or baseball bat and four stumps. Set up the wicket with two stumps about 1m apart, the third stump about 6-7m away to the left, the fourth stump is where the bowler bowls from – about 6m in front of the wicket. The bowler must bowl underarm and full toss. If you hit the ball you must run wherever the ball has gone. You run round the stump to the left and back to score one run. The bowler bowls as soon as he/she has the ball back. You are out if it goes through the wicket, or is caught, or if you are hit twice you are l.b.w. Any age can play; if the teams are small everyone can field and take turns to bat.

Theme 3: Musical games

Musical games are especially suitable for indoor games during winter time. Basically for these games you need good pop music the children can move around to. When the music stops they have to do something, the last to do so drops out.

1. **Musical bumps** When the music stops the children sit down.

2. **Musical statues** When the music stops the children have to freeze and stay still; if they move they are out.

3. **Musical chairs** Have a row of chairs facing alternate ways, one less than the total number of children playing. The children move round and have to sit down when the music stops. Take a chair away each time, until one child is left.

4. **Musical mats** Have old magazines or equivalent spread round the floor, one less than the number of children. When the music stops the children have to stand on a mat, the child without is out. Take a mat away each time.

5. **Musical stations** You need about 5 to 6 leaders standing on chairs around the room; whilst the music plays you tell them a number. When the music stops the children gather round the leaders who can only have the number of children you have told them, the rest have to go to another station. Any surplus children are out. Each time give your leaders a different number. TIP: this is good for large numbers of children.

Theme 4: Hall/Club games

1. **Traffic lights** The children move around the hall doing different things according to the colour you call out: RED means stop, GREEN means run, AMBER means walk, BLUE means jump, YELLOW means hop. If you call TRAFFIC LIGHTS the children line up in front of you, the last to do so is out.

2. **Beans** The children move around the hall doing different things according to the bean you call out. JUMPING BEANS means jump. RUNNER BEANS means run, DWARF BEANS means make yourself small and move close to the floor, BROAD BEANS means make yourself wide and move like a giant, FROZEN BEANS means stand still, FRENCH BEANS means go round holding hands together in front of you and saying 'Ooh la la', CHILI BEANS means going round with hand to mouth saying 'Hot'. If you call BAKED BEANS the children have to sit down, the last to do so is out.

3. **Fruit and veg** Line the children up in the middle of the room. Name one side of room FRUIT, one side VEGETABLE. You call out different fruit or veg, the children run to whichever side of the room is appropriate, the last there is out.

4. **Airports** Put up about 10 cards around the room which have the name of an airport. The children move round the room, and when you call out one of the airport names they have to line up at that airport. The last there is out. You can make up a story as you go bringing in the different places.

5. **Cops and robbers** A cop and robber are selected from the children, the rest form lines and hold hands, these are the streets and alleyways. The cop chases the robber up and down the streets. Every so often the leader calls CHANGE at which point the street players make a quarter turn and hold hands again, changing the direction of the streets. The two chasing each other are not allowed to break through the lines and have to adjust to running in a different direction. Take turns to be the cop and robber.

6. **Ladders** Divide into two teams. The teams sit opposite each other with feet touching the opposite team member. You need about 1m between each pair of children. Number down the line. When you call a number those children have to race each other, down the line of children, round to outside of the 'ladder', back down the middle to their own place. Establish which way to run first and tell the children to jump over legs not on them, hence the need for space between each pair. The first back scores a point for their team. Repeat until all have had a go.

Theme 5: Party games

1. **Drawing clumps** This is like Pictionary™. Divide into teams. Each team needs paper and pencils and a place to draw. You have a list of objects (Greens), or TV programmes or pop songs, etc. (Reds). Each

team sends one person to you, you give them the first object/subject to go back and draw for their team to guess. *No talking or writing allowed*. When the team has guessed it, they send someone else to come to you to tell you the answer and to be told the next topic to draw. The winner is the team that completes their list first.

2. **Miming clumps** As above except the teams have to mime, not draw.

3. **Copy monkey** Sit in a circle and send one child out. Choose a leader; that person does an action which everyone else copies. The leader keeps changing the action. The child who went out comes back and has to work out who the leader is. The leader then goes out.

4. **Twos and threes** You need chairs (enough for every child plus one more) randomly set out in groups of three round the room. The children sit on the chairs, apart from one pair that have a spare seat in their group of three chairs. Whilst you play music the two get up holding hands and grab a child from a group of three and sit back down. The new pair (because their third member has been taken) then do the same, and so on. When the music stops the pair at the time drop out, plus the child who was last taken, in order to have a new pair to start the game again.

5. **Hunt the teddy** (Greens) You need a soft toy such as a teddy. One child goes out and the rest hide the teddy. The child comes back to find it; they can be helped by saying HOT when they are near, and COLD when they are not near. Repeat with other children going out.

One more idea: Big equipment

If funds allow, you may like to hire a bouncy castle or a ball pond or other such equipment for one day. You need to take turns and watch safety rules carefully. Usually a five-minute turn followed by a rest works well.

GATE 3
CRAFT SESSIONS

Craft sessions

These sessions are very important. They give an opportunity to relax with the children, to get to know them. Children will talk as they are working. Some children, who find academic stuff boring or hard, really enjoy art and craft work and find success in this area. Most children are doers and love to make things. Craft can also provide opportunity to co-operate and work as a group to fulfil a task. You want activities that the children can do themselves, not too directed but giving a feeling of satisfaction at the end. The tasks need to be able to be completed in the time available. You need to be organised and ready for each day.

Here are suggestions for craft activities which you can choose from. You may want one activity each day that every group does or you may want a variety of activities each day that the groups rotate round over the week. Some of these tasks are more suitable for either Greens or Reds, some could be for both and these are listed first. There is a suggestion for an ongoing activity which lasts all week. Select different groups each day to work on this.

Tasks suitable for all ages

1. An airport (ongoing)

Product A model airport, scenery and runways, which an be displayed at the end of week.

All you need Toy planes, hardboard to build on, as big as you want, maybe 300cm by 100cm, a table to put it on, newspaper, glue, sellotape, stapler, marker pen, paints, boxes and junk modelling type material, corks, cocktail sticks, card, tissue paper in different colours, white paper such as lining paper, green crêpe paper, brown paper, felt tips.

Step 1   Glue lining paper onto the hardboard. Draw on runways and work out what scenery you want, i.e. hills, fields, sea, airport buildings.

Step 2   Paint the lining paper, grey for runways, blue, green or brown for other parts depending on your design.

Step 3   Build up hills by screwing up newspaper into balls which you pile up to the height you want. Cover these with lining paper which you then glue down. Staple as well to make sure it's secure. Paint appropriate colours, i.e. green, brown, purple, etc.

Step 4   Make the sea, if in your design, using blue tissue paper or blue material, again staple and glue down.

Step 5   Make trees using corks as base, cut tree shapes from card, push cocktail sticks through card then put into cork. Use little pieces of green tissue paper glued on for leaves.

Step 6   Make airport buildings using small grocery boxes such as tea or cereal boxes. Cover boxes in brown paper, use card folded in half and glued on to be roofs. With felt tips add windows and doors, paint roofs and other parts of houses if required.

Step 7 Make grass from green crêpe paper by cutting the paper still folded, into 4cm lengths, then cut along edge to give frayed effect. Glue down overlapping to give grass effect. Make flowers from twists of tissue paper, glue in place.

Step 8 Add whatever else you feel needed; such as clay people and toy planes.

You build this up over the week, groups doing different parts for it.

2. Banners (this can also be ongoing each day)

Product A banner depicting the memory verse for the day in collage – this is a group activity.

All you need Paper, felt tips, piece of plain coloured material, about 120cm by 100cm, letter templates, scrap materials, felt, scissors, material glue, other collage materials, e.g feathers, glitter, sequins, two garden canes, at least 120cm, needle and cotton.

Step 1 Write out the verse on paper for the group to work from.

Step 2 Using the letter templates the group cut out the letters for the verse. Then lay the letters on the material to see how to fit them. Glue in place.

Step 3 Decorate round the verse using the other collage material. Tip: for the younger groups you may need to shorten the verses or cut out the letters beforehand.

Step 4 Turn over the top and bottom of the banner, about 4cm, and stitch or glue to give a hem. Thread the canes through these hems so you can hang the banners. Tie a length of string to both ends of the top cane to be a loop for hanging with.

3. In-flight food

Product Filled rolls and iced buns.

All you need Rolls, fillings such as cheese spread, paste, jam, margarine or butter, little plain cakes, icing sugar, colouring or chocolate flavouring, i.e. cocoa, chocolate drops, knives, paper to cover tables, containers for the completed food such as foil trays, cling film, labels and pencils.

Step 1 Wash hands. Give each child a container to put the food in and a label to write their name on and put on the container. If you cover the table with clean paper the children can work directly on the table.

Step 2 Make the icing (water based) either with the children or make it beforehand; add colouring if wanted or flavour with chocolate. Each child has a plain bun which they ice and decorate with chocolate drops. Leave to dry.

Step 3 Each child has a roll which they spread and fill with own choice of filling.

Step 4 When completed the children cover the roll and cake in cling film and put in their container to take home.

If you have the facilities you may like to make the buns the first day with the children and then decorate the next.

4. Clay models

Product A plane model or other in clay.

All you need Modelling clay (preferably quick-drying variety especially for craft that does not need firing), knives and plastic tools to model with, aprons, bowls for water, card to put models on, pencils, plastic sheeting for tables and for floor, washing bowl, soap and towels to wash hands afterwards.

Step 1 Give each child a card for the base and ask them to write their name on.

Step 2 Give each child a lump of clay about the size of a mug. Show the children how to wet their fingers only in the water to help smooth the clay. Be careful not to get too much water on the clay, you need only a little.

Step 3 The children make whatever model they want to. When it's complete they put it on their card and place in a suitable area to dry. Tip: this needs to be left a day before they can take it home and is not an activity for the last day.

Step 4 Wash hands in the washing bowl and throw the water outside, not down the sink, clay can block up the pipes.

5. Models

Product A simple plane.

All you need Thin cardboard tubes cut into 10cm lengths, card, scissors, paints and brushes, felt tips, glue, templates for wing, nose and tail pieces.

Cut out paper shapes for decorating:

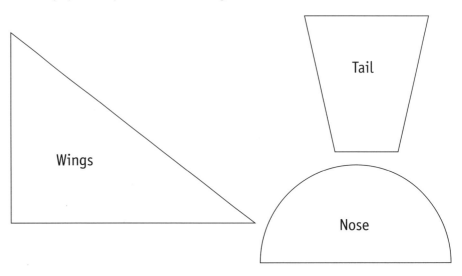

Step 1 Give each child a cardboard tube to be the centre of their plane. You can make a tube by rolling card and gluing or taping down.

Step 2 The children cut out wings, tail pieces and a nose for their model from card or you could cut these out ready beforehand.

Step 3 Attach the tail by cutting 2 slits either side down the end of the tube about 1 cm long and gluing into the slits.

Step 4 Make the nose into a cone shape and glue or tape together. Glue the inside of the cone and stuff with tissue paper. Put glue on the tissue paper and round the outside of the tube and stick the nose onto the plane base.

Step 5 Glue the wings on to the top of the tube.

Step 6 Paint or colour the models with felt tips. Add any decoration: windows, logos, etc. by gluing on the cut-out shapes or by drawing on.

Tasks suitable for Greens (5-7)

6. Aeroplane pictures

Product Painted picture framed.

All you need Outlines of a plane or helicopter, one per child, on A4 or A5 paper, paints, brushes, aprons, glue, strips of coloured card for frames (corrugated card is effective), card for backing same size as pictures, scissors, wool, tape.

Step 1 Each child paints in the plane outline.

Step 2 Stick the picture onto the backing card.

Step 3 Glue strips of card round the edge of the picture to make the frame. These need to overlap at corners then be trimmed square.

Step 4 Tape a loop of wool about 2cm at the top middle point of the frame so the picture can be hung.

7. Hot-air balloons

Product Baskets attached to a balloon.

All you need Balloons, string or wool, felt tips; either plastic tubs such as margarine tubs and paper and glue, or card to make into baskets; hole punch, small netting such as used to pack oranges.

Step 1 Children make a basket first. If you use the plastic tubs children need to cover the tubs by gluing on plain paper, then decorate with felt tips. If you use card you need A5 size per basket, draw a margin 4cm down each side. Fold each margin up towards centre and score, cut down at corners to margin one side only, as in diagram, cutting down the arrows.

Cut down
these arrows to margin

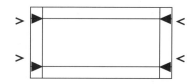

Bend up sides along score lines, fold the corners in and glue to make basket shape. Decorate with felt tips.

Step 2 Punch 4 holes evenly around edge of baskets. Attach string of equal lengths to these holes.

Step 3 Blow up a balloon and cover with netting, tie firmly round the knot of the balloon. Attach the basket to base of balloon. To hang up the balloon tie a loop of string to the netting which can be used as a handle or used to hang the balloon from a hook. The balloon can be decorated with felt tips (with care) before you attach the netting.

8. Windmills

Product A turning windmill on a stick.

All you need Squares of paper about 20cm in length, preferably coloured and strong but not heavy; thin green garden sticks, split pins, plastic straw cut into 5mm sections; small circles about 4cm diameter in card; tape, felt tips, scissors.

Step 1 Each child decorates their paper with felt tips in their own design.

Step 2 Fold the paper diagonally both ways and score, then reopen.

   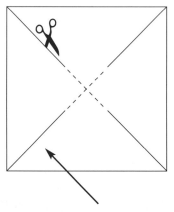

Step 3 The children cut down the diagonal lines to about 2cm from the centre.

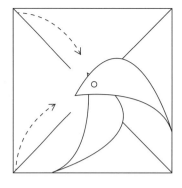

Step 4 Fold alternate halves of the corners into the centre so they overlap each other, leaving the other half open. Use a split pin to go through the corners in the centre of the square and into the centre of the small circle of card. Take out the pin and put the round section of the straw through that hole then replace the split pin going through the straw, bend back the pin to hold it together. This should allow the windmill to turn.

Step 5 Tape the card onto the green stick, making sure the windmill is free to turn. Blow on it or take it outside in the wind!

9. Mosaics

Product Picture filled in with small paper shapes.

All you need A4 paper; different coloured paper cut into small pieces; glue, pencils; selection of outlines such as planes, helicopters, cars, trees, flowers, rabbits, cats, etc. drawn on A4.

Step 1 The children could draw their own picture on A4 paper or choose a prepared outline.

Step 2 Fill in the pictures by sticking on small pieces of paper to make a mosaic. You can use many different sorts of paper – shiny, foil, wrapping paper, crêpe, wallpaper, etc.

Step 3 You could add strips of card round the edge as in Task 6 (Greens).

10. In-flight entertainment

Product Shadow puppets.

All you need White sheet, strong light; templates for puppet outlines such as people, animals, trees; card (old cereal boxes are suitable for this); sticks or old pencils, tape, scissors.

Step1 The children can choose what puppet they want to make. They draw round the outline onto card, cut it out and then attach it to a stick with tape.

Step 2 Set up the shadow theatre by hanging the white sheet from the ceiling. Shine the light onto it from the back. The children hold the puppet in the light to form a shadow on the sheet.

Step 3 Divide the group into two. Each group make up a story to 'enact' with their puppets to the other group who are now the audience. They then swap over.

Tasks suitable for Reds (8-11)

11. Sky pictures

Product Mixed medium picture on watercolour base.

All you need White A4 paper; watercolour paints such as poster paints; brushes, aprons, scissors, glue, additional collage materials such as scrap paper, old magazines, scrap material.

Step 1 The children select appropriate sky colours and make different colour washes by diluting a little paint with water. This needs to be very thin and painted thinly. They need to decide what sort of sky, e.g. whether it's a stormy sky, a sunset sky, summer's day sky or night sky and select colours accordingly. Each child needs about three washes, for instance – for a stormy sky: grey, yellow and dark blue; for night: grey, dark blue and purple; for sunset: orange, pink and red or yellow; for summer: two different blues and yellow.

Step 2 The children paint all over their piece of white paper using the three washes until it is completely covered. The wash should be thinly applied and should then dry very quickly.

Step 3 The children complete the picture by using collage to create a sky scene so they may want to add stars, birds, clouds, planes, anything that flies! They cut these out of the collage material available and glue it on. The background should be dry enough to glue on to.

Step 4 You could add a frame as in Task 6 (Greens).

12. Paper aeroplanes

Product Model plane.

All you need Sheets of A4 paper, preferably in striking colours, felt tips, scissors.

Step 1 Fold your piece of A4 paper in half. Make a mark 20cm down the outer edges and score both sides of the paper as shown.

Step 2 Open the paper and fold one corner along the scored line.

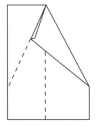

Step 3 Repeat with the other corner, folding back any paper that overlaps.

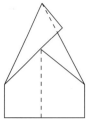

Step 4 Score across the top and fold over.

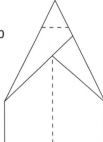

Step 5 Fold the paper in half and score two more lines.

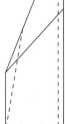

Step 6 Bend the paper over in opposite directions, and cut two snips as shown.

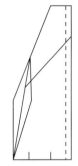

Step 7 Open the paper out again and launch it. Holding it at the back edge, put your forefinger on top and your other fingers underneath. Point the plane in the right direction and move your hand forward, letting the plane go. Adjust the elevators up if it dives or glides too steeply.

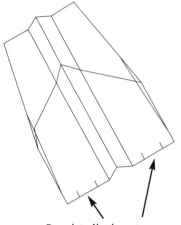

Bend tail elevators up

Step 8 Go to a large space such as church or even outside and have a competition to see whose goes the furthest. You may want to give a small prize or let the children demonstrate their plane at the final Runway.

13. Kites

Product A decorative kite.

All you need Diamond-shape paper about 30cm long, paints or felt tips or collage materials and glue, different coloured thin ribbon to make bows, wool, art straws cut to length of diamond-shape paper, tape.

Step 1 The children decorate their kites in designs of their own either with paints, felt tips or collage material. Alternatively use gift paper and have different designs the children can choose from.

Step 2 Cut the straws so that they can form a support structure, make a cross shape by twisting straws together and tape at join. Glue or tape the kite to the straws.

Step 3 Tie wool about 30cm long from bottom of stick to trail. Attach four bows to this wool using pieces of ribbon. Attach wool to the cross so that the kite can be hung up.

14. In-flight entertainment

This is a drama workshop and there are some ideas listed here to select from and develop.

All you need Any props you think helpful.

1. Drama game Stand in circle, one person moves across circle saying another person's name and goes to take their place. Before they get there that person has to start moving, say another persons' name and take their place, and that person then has to continue in same way. Check you all know each other's names before you start.

You can add doing an action that the person you name has to copy then add their own action as they move across the circle.

2. Mime Have cards with different airport-related jobs written on, such as pilot, steward, baggage handler, check-in operator, security, customs officer, shopkeeper, etc. The group members take turns to pick a card and then mime to others to guess.

3. Sketches Have cards with different places around the airport written on. The children work in pairs and have to talk to each other giving clues about where they are but not saying and again the rest have to guess. The places could be: in the cockpit, on the landing gear, on the tail of the plane, inside a case in the hold, inside a case being taken out to the plane, on an escalator, in an in-flight food tray, in the drinks trolley, inside a passport, in the security X-ray machine, inside a bus going out to the plane, etc.

4. Charades Divide into threes or fours. Let each group choose an airport as their word for charades. The group has to act a sketch to include each syllable of the word then a final sketch that gives the whole word. The sketches therefore require speaking. For instance Heathrow would be heath and row separately and then Heathrow. You may need to suggest airports such as East Midlands, Birmingham, Stansted, Gatwick, JFK, Paris.

5. Play-acting Use the scripts from the puppet plays and get the children to act these out. Some can read the parts whilst the others act it out. The children can do it like a play reading, reading their own part as they act out. You will need several copies of the scripts.

6. Shadow acting To make it seem more like a screen production you could do shadow acting by setting up a white sheet suspended from the ceiling with a strong light shining onto it from behind. You act in between the light and the sheet so that the audience see your shadow. Activity 2 or the play-acting would work well this way.

15. Fly-a-kite challenge

Product A kite.

All you need Plastic sheeting (bin bags cut open), sticks such as green gardening sticks, staplers, tape, string, glue, scissors, rulers and pens.

Step 1 Set the children a challenge to design and make a kite that flies. They may want to work in pairs.

Step 2 Show them the materials you have and tell them to have a go at creating a kite. Give them a time limit and allow time to go outside and see if any will fly.

Step 3 If anyone succeeds you may like to give them either a prize or a certificate.

NAME: _____

Fly-a-kite challenge
Well done!
Your kite flew!

BOGGLES & CO.

Production notes

Cast

Boggles The 'hero', in his 20s or 30s, needs to be fairly agile to do some of the slapstick routines.

Grasper Frederick Arthur Grasper, owner of FAG *(NB. Could be Fiona Arabella Grasper)*. The prototypical 'villain' – perhaps a little older than Boggles. Smartly dressed, superior, sneering voice.

Vanya Young woman, the 'heroine', speaks with a foreign accent, except for the last day when she speaks with no accent.

Mrs Farquason-Smythe (Only in the longer version of the play). Older, 'upper-class' lady.

The set

The scene is a small airport. This could be a painted canvas backcloth, in the style of theatres past. It may be easier (and cheaper) to make a set, using at least four 8ft x 4ft sheets of hardboard, suitably framed ('flats' as they are called). These could be joined together – even hinged for easy storage and handling – and able to stand in the style of a large clothes-horse. However, it is very important to have it secure to prevent it falling over. Ask your local amateur dramatic society for advice. Such a set would also enable you to have entry and exit points around the sides.

Paint the 'flats' plain magnolia, perhaps decorated with travel posters and publicity material from your local airport? (See notes of props for individual episodes.)

Light and sound

The important thing is that children can both see and hear what is going on. This means generally having some kind of stage, which is recommended for the holiday club anyway.

Hiring three radio mics is the best way of enabling the cast to be heard (there is never a time when all four cast members are on stage at once). If the cost of this is prohibitive, consider recording the play earlier, then miming to the recording – a method that is especially useful when children are involved, who may be even more prone to forgetting lines. Do a good job with the audio recording, remembering to leave enough empty spaces when the action is taking place. (Practical note: Beware recording equipment that has automatic level control. It will 'hunt' for a sound during the silences, which means a loud hissing sound.)

This method may sound inferior, but it does mean that if someone forgets a line, all they have to do is move their lips! In my experience, children are too caught up in the story to notice if the miming is inaccurate!

Day 1: Vanya arrives in the Governor's country

Theme: Kingdom love

Jesus said, 'My command is this: love each other as I have loved you.' (John 15:12, NIV)

Scene

Airport A smart desk, complete with computer, 'Passport Processing Machine' (complete with flashing lights etc.). Smart sign with FAST AIRLINE GROUP (FAG).

Props list

FAG desk This is a table, clad with suitably painted hardboard to make it look like a modern check-in desk at an airport. It stands to the right. (See note below about the computer.)

FAG sign FAST AIRLINE GROUP (FAG). This should be smart-looking – use a computer to help create this. The sign should be fixed above or near the desk.

Computer Use an old or inoperative monitor and keyboard for this. The monitor faces away from the audience, and so it does not matter if it is non-functioning. Stand it on the FAG desk, with an obvious slit on the front of the desk from which lots of paper will emerge when required. Have a slot on the top of the desk for inserting a single sheet of paper. Either use a helper underneath the desk (who can also make the appropriate rude noises), or rig some method for Boggles to 'secretly' release lots of paper from the lower slot.

Swivel chair Behind desk.

Passport processing machine This is simply a suitably painted box which also sits on the desk. Have one or two flashing lights on it (Christmas lights?) when it 'works'. Audience only sees the back, so most of the action can be sheer pretence.

Paper For the computer.

Arrival card Vanya has this – it can actually be blank, but probably better with some printing on it. The audience will not see this in detail.

The play

Boggles is behind the desk, fiddling with the computer. Frederick Arthur Grasper, owner of FAG, is peering over his shoulder. (NB. The character could be Fiona Arabella Grasper.)

Boggles It's no good, Mr Grasper, I'm no good with these new-fangled things. I'm a pilot, and that's where I should be – up in the air!

Grasper   Well, you're not in the air, Boggles. I'm not going to let you loose on one of my beautiful airliners. You'll learn to operate the computer or lose your job!

Boggles   Well, don't blame me if anything goes wrong. I'm trying my best.

Grasper   I want more than your best, Boggles. We are the *FAG* and this airline is the best and most modern in the country. We also have to check the passports of all arrivals, and stamp any visas. I had to get this equipment to do the job, and it cost me a fortune, and so I want my money's worth from it.

[Computer makes rude noise]

Boggles   Sorry – that was the computer, not me. Look, when I put this piece of paper in here, it should print out nicely, but look what it does. *[Places paper in machine, but paper flies all over the place]*

Grasper   Oh – tidy it up, Boggles – but don't think this gets you off – you'll do this or do nothing!

Boggles   You mean . . .

Grasper   I mean you'll be out of a job!

[Computer makes another rude noise]

[Vanya enters. Grasper tidies himself up and puts on exaggerated smile]

Grasper   Yes, Madam, what can I do for you? You have come to the desk of the FAST AIRLINE GROUP, and I am Grasper – Frederick Arthur Grasper, the owner of the airline. You wish to fly to an exotic country – a well-deserved holiday, perhaps?

Vanya   *[Speaks with foreign accent]* No . . .

Grasper   A flight across the mountains to visit family on the other side of the Governor's country?

Vanya   No. My name is Vanya and I have just arrived in your country.

Grasper   Oh, then please may I have your passport?

Vanya   I have no passport. But I do have an arrival card . . .

Grasper   Here, Boggles, see what you can do with this, and process the lady's arrival.

[Boggles takes card and has trouble trying to make the machine work]

Vanya   Please, I am looking for a job in your 'FANCY AIRLINE GROUP'.

Grasper   *FAST* AIRLINE GROUP, Miss. Mind you, we pride ourselves at being ultra smart and 'fancy', don't we, Boggles?

[Computer makes another rude noise. Grasper is annoyed but examines arrival card]

Grasper   Oh. *[Disappointed – attitude changes]* I see that you are from the country of Banandra. Well, of course, *that* is why you have no passport, and without a valid passport I feel I cannot give you a visa to enter the Governor's country. I regret that those from Banandra generally don't fit in here!

Vanya   I am sorry . . . I . . .

Grasper   *[Checks the computer screen]* And our records show that you have no merit points and don't deserve to enter . . . You are just not suitable for the Governor's country!

Boggles   You hypocrite, Grasper! I was in this airport when *you* arrived here only a few years ago! You had no passport either – and the records showed some things about your life that made *you* very unsuitable and unworthy to enter the Governor's country!

Grasper   But that was a long time ago. Things have changed . . .

Boggles   But the Governor has not changed. He still grants a passport to any who would receive one.

Grasper   But *he* isn't here, is he? As owner of the Airline Desk, *I* have the responsibility to grant entry visas. I want this country to stay clean and pure, not crowded with unsuitable people.

Boggles   What gives you the right to judge? And what about showing the same compassion the Governor showed us when we arrived?

Grasper   You can't show compassion to *anybody*! Now if this person had more merit points, she might deserve more compassion, but . . .

Boggles   Deserve compassion?? If that's your attitude, I'm quitting! You can keep your FAG, Grasper! I'm going to start a new airline – Boggles Flying Company – straightaway!

Grasper   You can't do that! You haven't any planes!

Boggles   I'll borrow one when I need it. Meanwhile, as an official new airline – and this is my airline desk – I can process new arrivals to the Governor's country. Miss Vanya, the Governor granted Grasper and I passports when we arrived – he just loves all who come to him and his country, and so I can give you a visa, and promise you a passport.

Grasper   Love! What's love got to do with it?

Boggles   If you really knew the Governor, you'd know that it matters a lot! Anyway, Miss Vanya, I welcome you as a new citizen of the Governor's country!

Vanya   Oh, thank you so much, Captain Boggles.

Boggles   Oh, just call me Boggles, everyone does. And if you still want a job, you can work for BFC – Boggles Flying Company!

Vanya   Oh yes, please!

Grasper   You're stupid, Boggles! You can't – you shouldn't . . . Well, you won't survive for long. You can't just give away passports – you're making it too easy. Just wait until the Governor hears about this. Then FAG will have the last laugh!

[Computer makes another rude noise as they all exit]

Day 2: The Boggles Flying Company

Theme: Kingdom justice

Jesus said, 'Father, forgive them, for they don't know what they are doing.' (Luke 23:34, NIV)

Scene

Airport The FAST AIRLINE GROUP (FAG). Smart desk, stands next to the BOGGLES FLYING COMPANY (BFC) desk which is very shabby, untidy, with hand-written signs etc.

Props list

FAG desk and sign As in Day 1.

Computer As in Day 1 with addition of a mouse.

Passport processing machine As in Day 1.

Swivel chair As in Day 1.

Old table Old, but solid.

BFC sign Rough hand-written sign with string for hanging up.

Pot of paint, small brush.

Letter.

Box Simple cardboard box – more BFC 'Office Equipment'.

BFC badges An attempt at some kind of 'uniform'.

Shirt in packaging.

Duplicate shirt (able to be damaged). This is to be switched for the good shirt.

The play

The trouble Boggles experiences hanging his sign above his desk gives scope for much comedy. Boggles could borrow the swivel chair from Grasper, who looks on bemused. With careful practice (emphasis on careful) Boggles could stand on the chair to hang up his sign, with the chair moving about, apparently out of control. Of course, if you do this, you should warn the children afterwards not to copy, as it is dangerous. Some may feel that for this reason this should be omitted, perhaps with some other fun way for Boggles to hang his sign – be creative!

The story so far *(possibly spoken by a narrator)*
Vanya, a citizen of Banandra, has arrived in the Governor's country. At first she was refused entry to the country by Frederick Arthur Grasper, owner of the FAST AIRLINE GROUP, who claimed she was unsuitable for the Governor's country and could not have a passport. Boggles, a pilot, was angry at this, and instantly formed BFC – the BOGGLES FLYING COMPANY. This meant that under the laws of the country, he could grant entry to Vanya, and promise her a passport from the Governor, who loves all who come to him and his country. This has not pleased Grasper.

Grasper is smart and calm behind his desk. Boggles enters with package and BFC sign. Struggles to put the sign up above his desk.

Grasper   You call yourself an airline? With no planes – I mean not even *one* plane!

Boggles   Well, give us a few days, and we'll see who is a proper airline, Grasper. Look – we have our desk, and I have an official badge . . . and look, I've spent my savings on a special uniform shirt. *[Takes shirt out of package, places on desk]*

Grasper   It takes more than a uniform to make an airline – people will laugh at you!

Boggles   I don't think so – you may have the smart machinery, but I have the friendly face that welcomes all to the Governor's country!

Grasper   A friendly face you may have, but that's all! I've reported you to the Governor. When he hears about your behaviour, promising passports to people who don't deserve one, you'll be in trouble, you'll see!

Boggles   Well, we'll see, Grasper. Meanwhile, I have some more things to pick up for the desk.

Grasper   Hmph! *[Boggles exits, Grasper works at his computer. Vanya enters opposite side, carrying a small pot of paint and a brush]*

Vanya   Good morning, Mr Grasper! How are you today?

Grasper   Hmph! *[Pretents to ignore Vanya, as she proceeds to put finishing touches to Boggles' table]*

[Computer mouse falls from Grasper's desk]

Grasper   Oh tish! That's my mouse!

Vanya   A mouse! *[Screams, spills paint]*

Grasper   No not a live mouse – my computer mouse. Don't they teach you anything in Banandra?

Vanya   Your computer mouse? Oh, but it just frightened me. Oh, look at the mess!

Grasper   Here, use this to wipe up the mess. *[With malicious grin hands Boggles' shirt to Vanya, who uses it to wipe up the paint, even ripping it, etc. Boggles enters, carrying box and letter]*

Boggles   Hello Vanya! Here, Grasper, a letter for you. Vanya, is everything all right?

Vanya   Not quite, I just had a small fright, and spilt some paint, but I've managed to wipe it up with this bit of cloth.

Boggles   Good. There's no harm done. Vanya, I managed to use all my savings on a top-quality shirt as a posh uniform. Have you seen it? *[They look around, while Grasper smirks]* Hang on, what's this? *[Picks up damaged shirt]* This looks like . . . it *is* . . . it *was* my new uniform shirt! Vanya, what have you done?

Vanya   What do you mean, Boggles?

Boggles   This 'bit of cloth' was my brand-new uniform shirt!

Vanya   Oh, Boggles, I am so sorry . . . I did not know . . . I just . . . *[She is upset]*

Grasper   *[Grasper takes Boggles to one side]* You see, Boggles, you can't trust these people from Banandra – low intelligence – couldn't tell the difference between a new shirt and a paint rag!

[Grasper returns to desk to examine letter]

Boggles   It's all right, Vanya. Like Grasper said, the BFC is more than a smart uniform – even if it did cost me my savings!

Vanya   Oh, I *am* sorry . . .

Boggles   Yes, I know, and as I said, it really is OK! Go and wipe your tears away. I'm not angry – I'm not exactly happy – but I'm not angry. Our friendship is much more important.

Vanya   Oh, Boggles, you are so kind. *[Exits]*

Grasper   Is there no justice?

Boggles   What do you mean?

Grasper   You forgive an idiot of a girl who ruins an expensive shirt, and the Governor says you are perfectly right to grant a passport to her! He says 'Each Passport is uniquely made and delivered by special courier to the issuing airline, who will hand it to the new citizen'!

Boggles   I won't say 'I told you so', but . . .

Grasper   'Uniquely made' . . . 'delivered by courier' – who pays for these passports given away so freely to undesirable people? I suppose it comes out of our taxes!

Boggles   Actually, the Governor pays for each of these himself. They are his personal gift to the citizens of the country. And he doesn't take it lightly – it is part of a great Covenant made in old times.

Grasper   He should be more choosy!

Boggles   But he is choosy – he chooses people who don't deserve a passport, and gives one freely – that's how you and I got ours, Grasper, remember? And by the way, why didn't you stop Miss Vanya using my new shirt as a paint rag?

Grasper   I, I, I . . .

Boggles   It's all right, Grasper. I forgive you, too. You don't deserve it, but that's the way things are in the Governor's country!

Grasper   I suppose I should thank you.

Boggles   Yes, but instead, you can do me just one small favour . . .

[Exit]

Day 2: The Boggles Flying Company

(SHORT PROGRAMME VERSION)

Theme: Kingdom justice

Jesus said, 'Father, forgive them, for they don't know what they are doing.' (Luke 23:34, NIV)

Scene

Airport The FAST AIRLINE GROUP (FAG). Smart desk, stands next to the BOGGLES FLYING COMPANY (BFC) desk which is very shabby, untidy, with hand-written signs etc.

Props list

FAG desk and sign As in Day 1.

Computer As in Day 1 with addition of a mouse.

Passport processing machine As in Day 1.

Swivel Chair As in Day 1.

Old table Old, but solid.

BFC sign Rough hand-written sign with string for hanging up.

Pot of paint, small brush.

Letter.

Box Simple cardboard box – more BFC 'Office Equipment'.

BFC badges An attempt at some kind of 'uniform'.

Shirt in packaging.

Duplicate shirt (able to be damaged). This is to be switched for the good shirt.

The play

The trouble Boggles experiences hanging his sign above his desk gives scope for much comedy. Boggles could borrow the swivel chair from Grasper, who looks on bemused. With careful practice (emphasis on careful) Boggles could stand on the chair to hang up his sign, with the chair moving about, apparently out of control. Of course, if you do this, you should warn the children afterwards not to copy, as it is dangerous. Some may feel that for this reason this should be omitted, perhaps with some other fun way for Boggles to hang his sign – be creative!

The story so far *(possibly spoken by a narrator)*
Vanya, a citizen of Banandra, has arrived in the Governor's country. At first she was refused entry to the country by Frederick Arthur Grasper, owner of the FAST AIRLINE GROUP, who claimed she was unsuitable for the Governor's country and could not have a passport. Boggles, a pilot, was angry at this, and instantly formed BFC – the BOGGLES FLYING

COMPANY. This meant that under the laws of the country, he could grant entry to Vanya, and promise her a passport from the Governor, who loves all who come to him and his country. This has not pleased Grasper.

Grasper is smart and calm behind his desk. Boggles enters with package and BFC sign. Struggles to put the sign up above his desk.

Grasper	You call yourself an airline? With no planes – I mean not even *one* plane!
Boggles	Well, give us a few days, and we'll see who is a proper airline, Grasper. Look – we have our desk, and I have an official badge . . . and look, I've spent my savings on a special uniform shirt. *[Takes shirt out of package and places on desk]*
Grasper	It takes more than a uniform to make an airline – people will laugh at you!
Boggles	I don't think so – you may have the smart machinery, but I have the friendly face that welcomes all to the Governor's Country!
Grasper	A friendly face you may have, but that's all! There's a Government Inspection for all airlines, and you haven't a chance of passing it! I've reported you to the Governor. When he hears about your behaviour, promising passports to people who don't deserve one, you'll be in trouble, you'll see!
Boggles	Well, we'll see, Grasper. Meanwhile, I have some more things to pick up for the desk.
Grasper	Hmph!
	[Boggles exits, Grasper works at his computer. Vanya enters opposite side, carrying a small pot of paint and a brush]
Vanya	Good morning Mr Grasper! How are you today?
Grasper	Hmph! *[Pretents to ignore Vanya, as she proceeds to put finishing touches to desk]*
	[Computer mouse falls from Grasper's desk]
Grasper	Oh tish! That's my mouse!
Vanya	A mouse! *[Screams, spills paint]*
Grasper	No, not a live mouse – my computer mouse. Don't they teach you anything in Banandra?
Vanya	Your computer mouse? Oh, but it just frightened me. Oh look at the mess!
Grasper	Here, use this to wipe up the mess. *[With malicious grin, hands Boggles' shirt to Vanya, who uses it to wipe up the paint, even ripping it, etc. Boggles enters, carrying box and letter]*
Boggles	Hello Vanya! Here, Grasper, a letter for you. Vanya, is everything all right?
Vanya	Not quite, I just had a small fright, and spilt some paint, but I've managed to wipe it up with this bit of cloth.

Boggles   Good. There's no harm done. Vanya, I managed to use all my savings on a top-quality shirt as a posh uniform. Have you seen it? *[They look around, while Grasper smirks]* Hang on, what's this? *[Picks up damaged shirt]* This looks like . . . it *is* . . . it *was* my new uniform shirt! Vanya, what have you done?

Vanya   What do you mean, Boggles?

Boggles   This 'bit of cloth' was my brand-new uniform shirt!

Vanya   Oh, Boggles, I am so sorry . . .I did not know . . . I just . . . *[She is upset]*

Grasper   *[Grasper takes Boggles to one side]* You see, Boggles, you can't trust these people from Banandra – low intelligence – couldn't tell the difference between a new shirt and a paint rag!

[Grasper returns to desk to examine letter]

Boggles   It's all right, Vanya. Like Grasper said, the BFC is more than a smart uniform – even if it did cost me my savings!

Vanya   Oh, I *am* sorry . . .

Boggles   Yes, I know, and as I said, it really is OK! Go and wipe your tears away. I'm not angry – I'm not exactly happy – but I'm not angry. Our friendship is much more important.

Vanya   Oh, Boggles, you are so kind. *[Exits]*

Grasper   Is there no justice?

Boggles   What do you mean?

Grasper   You forgive an idiot of a girl who ruins an expensive shirt, and the Governor says you are perfectly right to grant a passport to her! He says 'Each Passport is uniquely made and delivered by special courier to the issuing airline, who will hand it to the new citizen'!

Boggles   I won't say 'I told you so', but . . .

Grasper   'Uniquely made' . . . 'delivered by courier' – who pays for these passports given away so freely to undesirable people? I suppose it comes out of our taxes!

Boggles   Actually, the Governor pays for each of these himself. They are his personal gift to the citizens of the country. And he doesn't take it lightly – it is part of a great Covenant made in old times.

Grasper   He should be more choosy!

Boggles   But he is choosy – he chooses people who don't deserve a passport, and gives one freely – thats how you and I got ours, Grasper, remember? And by the way, why didn't you stop Miss Vanya using my new shirt as a paint rag?

Grasper   I, I, I . . .

Boggles   It's all right, Grasper. I forgive you, too. You don't deserve it, but that's the way things are in the Governor's country!

[Exit]

Day 3: Good news for Grasper

Theme: Kingdom living

Jesus said, 'I have come in order that you may have life – life in all its fullness.' (John 10:10, *Good News Bible*)

Scene

Airport The FAST AIRLINE GROUP (FAG). Smart desk, stands next to the BOGGLES FLYING COMPANY (BFC) desk which is very shabby, untidy, with hand-written signs, etc.

Props list

FAG desk and sign As before.

Computer As before.

Passport processing machine As before.

Swivel chair As before.

Old table As before.

BFC sign As before.

Cake in box A paper plate, piled with shaving foam (at the last minute), and placed in a thin cake box. For more realism, use a basic sponge piled high with spray cream!

The play

The story so far (*possibly spoken by a narrator*)
Vanya, a citizen of Banandra, has arrived in the Governors' country. Boggles, a pilot, has set up his own airline – the BOGGLES FLYING COMPANY. Much to the annoyance of Frederick Arthur Grasper, owner of the FAST AIRLINE GROUP, who claimed she was unsuitable for the Governor's country, Boggles had enabled Vanya to receive a passport from the Governor. By a mean trick, Grasper tried to persuade Boggles to send Vanya back to her own country. This did not work, however, but Boggles forgave the mischievous Grasper. But in return, he had asked Grasper for just one small favour . . .

Grasper is smart and calm behind his desk. Boggles enters dressed for a flight – 'bomber' jacket, flying helmet, etc.

Boggles Well, I'm ready, Grasper. Thank you very much for the loan of your plane.

Grasper It's against my better judgement, but I suppose I had to return the favour, seeing as I was partly responsible for the ruin of your 'uniform shirt'.

Boggles We won't say any more about that, Grasper. 'Forgiven and forgotten' is one of the Governor's sayings, and I'm trying to copy it. Anyway, I'm really looking forward to this flight – I haven't been up in a plane for ages!

[Vanya enters]

Vanya What is happening, Boggles? I thought we haven't got a plane, but you are dressed to fly one.

Boggles Well, Vanya, our friend Mr Grasper has kindly loaned me one of his small planes for a short while!

Grasper Yes, and it occurs to me that it would be good for you to accompany him, Miss Vanya. You could practice your technique as a stewardess!

Boggles That's a good idea – we have to be flexible with our roles in the BOGGLES FLYING COMPANY.

Vanya *[Attracted by the glamour of being a stewardess]* Yes, that may be a good idea. *[Possible bit of fun doing the 'safety instructions']*

Boggles Well, it won't be as in big planes, Vanya, it's only a small plane, not one of Grasper's big passenger planes.

Vanya What do you mean? How small is the plane?

Boggles Well, look over there *[Points off-stage – Vanya looks]*

Vanya That is not a plane – it is only a few pieces of metal bolted together! I cannot go in that!

Grasper Of course you can, Miss Vanya! It is a perfectly good plane, and with a reliable experienced pilot like Boggles, you will be in very safe hands!

Vanya I am not sure.

Boggles Do come, Vanya. You can trust me – I won't let anything happen to you.

Vanya Oh, all right.

Boggles Come on, let's go, then. *[Exit. Grasper looks on with glee]*

Grasper Trust the pilot? I wouldn't trust that Boggles with a paper aeroplane! Mind you, that plane is such a heap of rubbish, none of my pilots will fly it any more. I'm sure Boggles will just about manage it, but it won't be at all pleasant! *[Chuckles]* That girl won't forget her trip with her new boss – she'll be either so sick or so angry she won't want to stay here in the Governor's country!

[Mrs Farquason-Smythe enters, carrying cake box]

Mrs F-S Mr Grasper?

Grasper Yes. How may I help you, Madam?

Mrs F-S It's more a case of how I can help you, Mr Grasper. My name is Farquason-Smythe – Felicity Farquason-Smythe. I understand you have applied to my company for a loan.

Grasper   Mrs Farquason-Smythe! Dear lady, please do take a seat. Forgive the untidy mess – this is the sad desk of a rival airline company. It lowers the tone of the place, but . . . may I take the box?

Mrs F-S   Yes. *[Takes seat – hands box carefully to Grasper]* Be careful with that. That box contains my best creation yet! *[Grasper looks puzzled]* It is a cake, Mr Grasper, but not just *any* cake. You see, that is my hobby . . .

Grasper   *[Looking at box, puzzled]* Mr Farquason-Smythe?

Mrs F-S   Not my *hubby*, my *hobby*, my passion. This afternoon is the great cake competition, and I am determined to win once more!

Grasper   How nice. *[Places box on BFC desk]*

Mrs F-S   But that is not why I am here. Mr Grasper, I understand that there is to be a Government inspection of the airport very soon.

Grasper   There is?

Mrs F-S   There is. I have it on good authority from my daughter's husband, who works in the appropriate department in Government House across the mountains.

Grasper   Well, thank you for telling me.

Mrs F-S   The point is, Mr Grasper, that the airline that passes the inspection will receive 'favoured status', and that being so I am willing to invest a *very* large sum of money.

Grasper   That is good news, Mrs Farquason-Smythe. I myself have invested heavily in FAG – the FAST AIRLINE GROUP. I believe so much in the future that I have spent everything I have on the latest state-of-the-art computerised equipment. In fact, there is nothing left. So the news of your investment fills me with delight!

Mrs F-S   The investment is not made yet, Mr Grasper. It is all subject to the inspection.

Grasper   Quite. Well, Mrs Farquason-Smythe, let me show you round. You will soon see that there is no competition, and that FAG will be the airline that gets your investment. *[Escorts Mrs F-S out – music to denote passing of time. Boggles and Vanya enter]*

Vanya   Boggles – that was wonderful! I should not have doubted your ability! You are an excellent pilot, and a rubbish heap like that plane of Grasper's is no problem to you!

Boggles   You're very kind! You can always trust an experienced pilot. Safety is the highest priority, and because of our friendship, I was bound to be doubly careful, and try and give you the best possible flight!

[Grasper enters]

Grasper Oh, you're back! I'm sorry, Miss Vanya, for the terrible time you must have had. I'm sure you realise now that the BOGGLES FLYING COMPANY is just a cowboy company, and that as there are no other jobs available, you may as well return to your own country as soon as . . .

Boggles What are you on about, Grasper?

Vanya Yes, I do not understand, Mr Grasper. I have had such a wonderful time! I was so worried that I was almost ill before I got into the plane. But then I realised I must trust the pilot, especially because I know him, and trust that he will always do what is best for me. And as a result, it was the most wonderful experience of my life!

Grasper I don't believe it. But anyway, I can't stay chatting. There is a box here that belongs to a visitor.

Boggles Is this it? *[Picks up box and begins to throw it. Vanya bends down to fix shoe]*

Grasper No! Don't throw it! *[Reaches out to take box. Vanya stands and knocks box – cake goes over Grasper]*

You idiots, both of you! Now I'll never get the money . . .

Boggles What money?

Grasper *[Realising mistake]* Money? Did I say money? No I said, 'I'll never fill my tummy!' Excuse me – I have to apologise to someone. *[Exits with cake remnants]*

Boggles What is he up to, I wonder? I find it hard to trust him, Vanya.

[Exit]

Day 3: Boggles is in a dilemma

(SHORT PROGRAMME VERSION)

Theme: Kingdom choices

Jesus said, 'The Holy Spirit, the Spirit of truth . . . will guide you into truth.' (John 16:13, NIV)

Scene

Airport The FAST AIRLINE GROUP (FAG). Smart desk, stands next to the BOGGLES FLYING COMPANY (BFC) desk which is very shabby, untidy, with hand-written signs, etc.

Props list

FAG desk and sign, with computer, passport machine, swivel chair, Boggles' 'desk' and sign All as before.

Telephone Could be a mobile phone.

Briefcase This is specially rigged to 'explode' in the final episode. Use some gold paint to paint an official-looking 'crest' on the case. It could be a nice-looking box, instead.

Robotic processing machine A large box, suitably painted, large enough for Vanya to crouch inside unseen. Mount it on castors to make it easier to drag on stage. Paint it grey and make it look rather 'electromechanical'! It should have an 'input' slot, a large 'output' slot, and a hole through which VANYA can squirt water at GRASPER. Add some kind of 'speaking tube'.

Paper For Boggles' trick on Grasper.

Envelope For Boggles' trick on Grasper.

Glass of water (on FAG desk) For Boggles' trick on Grasper.

Water pistol (or garden spray) For Boggles' trick on Grasper.

Flowerpots (small and large) For Boggles' trick on Grasper.

Matchboxes (small and large) For Boggles' trick on Grasper.

Governor's handbook A large (red?) hard-backed book.

Books and pages For Boggles to carry when he enters.

The play

The story so far (narrator)
Vanya, a citizen of Banandra, has arrived in the Governor's country. Boggles, a pilot, has set up his own airline – the BOGGLES FLYING COMPANY. Much to the annoyance of Frederick Arthur Grasper, owner of the FAST AIRLINE GROUP, who claimed she was unsuitable for the Governor's country, Boggles had enabled Vanya to receive a passport from the Governor. By a mean trick, Grasper tried to persuade Boggles to send Vanya back to her own

country. This did not work, however, and Boggles forgave the mischievous Grasper. But there is to be an inspection of the airlines, which may mean the end of one of them . . .

Grasper is smart and calm behind his desk. Phone rings and he answers it.

Grasper Good morning . . . Fast Airline Group . . . Frederick Grasper speaking. How may I help you? Oh, Mrs Farquason-Smythe. And how are things in the Governor's Inspection Department today? Yes, I know there is to be an inspection – you couldn't tell me when? No I suppose not. What? What's that you say? There is a large sum of money to be given to the airline that passes the inspection? How wonderful! Pardon? There will be some technical questions? What kind of technical questions? What? Worried? Me? No, of course not, dear lady, but thank you for the warning. I can look up the latest papers and things from the Governor – best to be prepared. Thank you for ringing. Goodbye. *[Puts phone down, stands up rubbing his hands with pleasure]* Well, a large sum of money for the successful airline, eh? I'll have to make sure that it's mine!

[Boggles enters with papers and books which fall all over the desk and onto the floor]

Grasper Just look at you! Boggles – I wouldn't even try, if I were you. You'll never pass the government inspection. You are a mockery of an airline! You have no planes, you have one employee – a highly unsuitable immigrant . . .

Boggles I'll get a plane when I need one, don't you worry, Grasper. As I've said before, you may have all the smart machinery, but I have the friendly face that welcomes all to the Governor's country!

Grasper Friendly face – pah! Listen, running an airline is serious business. Look, here I am with the latest computerised equipment for processing passports. All you have are a few pieces of paper and a pen . . .

Boggles Don't you worry, Grasper. You won't be the only one with computerised equipment. I've had a special delivery of a new robotic processing machine, so there!

Grasper A robotic processing machine? Just what is one of those? Oh don't bother – you're dreaming again, aren't you?

[Exits shaking his head in disbelief. Vanya enters carrying a box/briefcase – Boggles helps her – can have some difficulty trying to get it onto messy desk, etc.]

Boggles What's this, Vanya? Some more of your luggage?

Vanya No, I found it near the departure gate.

Boggles Right. Well, put it down and help me a minute.

[Exit while Grasper enters opposite side. After a few moments, Boggles enters dragging large box]

Grasper What *have* you got there?

Boggles I told you – it's my robotic processing machine.

Grasper And what is it supposed to do?

Boggles Just about anything. Look, it will type letters for me. *[Speaks into machine – machine makes noises, etc. Piece of paper comes out of slot, Grasper takes it and reads what Boggles dictated]*

Grasper I don't believe it!

Boggles It will even put the letter in an envelope and give it to me, ready to post! *[Puts paper into machine – out comes envelope]*

Grasper Hmmm.

Boggles It even enlarges things – look. *[Puts in small object – large object comes out – does this once or twice]*

Grasper I see. *[Realising he is being tricked]* Do you think it could enlarge a glass of water? *[Tips some water into machine but is squirted with a lot more! Boggles laughs as Grasper exits, and Vanya comes out of box laughing]*

Boggles Vanya, that was great!

Vanya It was fun, Boggles, but I hope it did not make Mr Grasper too angry.

Boggles No – he'll get over it!

Vanya Anyway, Boggles, what shall we do with this case I found? *[Picks up the briefcase]* Look – it has a special sign on it.

Boggles That's a government crest. Vanya, this must belong to a government official. Where did you say you found it?

Vanya By the departure gate. Whoever it belongs to must have flown out with FAG's morning flight an hour ago.

Boggles Well, it can't be one of our flights – we still haven't got a plane!

Vanya It looks very important.

Boggles I wonder. Vanya, do you think it belongs to a government observer?

Vanya What do you mean?

Boggles I mean, what if a government observer has already been to the airport, you know, an advance look at things, ready for the inspection?

Vanya Do you think so?

Boggles I do – and that case may contain some important information about the inspection!

Vanya What shall we do?

Boggles   We ought to return it to the owner, I guess. But I'd love to have just a little look inside. You know, that information could give us the edge over Grasper and FAG.

[Vanya produces large handbook]

Vanya   Let's see what the Handbook says . . .

Boggles   Oh, I know what it says.

Vanya   It says, 'Lost property must be treated with respect and confidence, as if it were still in the hands of the owner . . .'

Boggles   In other words, 'Hands off!' But still, I could just have a *little* look . . .

Vanya   No, Boggles. You know that would be against the Governor's wishes.

Boggles   Ah, but he isn't here, is he? And when the inspector comes . . .

[Grasper enters]

Grasper   . . . When the inspector comes he will see that FAG is the supreme airline, and that your poor excuse of a company will have to go!

[Vanya and Boggles groan and shake their heads]

Grasper   Hello, what have we here?

Vanya   It's some lost property.

Boggles   It's a government briefcase, Grasper, left by the departure gate.

Grasper   So I see . . .

Vanya   And Boggles thinks it may belong to an observer who's already come to look at the airport – a kind of advance inspection!

Grasper   Oh yes, I see what you mean. Well, if you let me take it, I can fly it over the mountains to Government House on the next flight.

Boggles   No – we'll just hang on to it for the moment.

Grasper   But you know what the Handbook says?

Vanya   Yes, it says that 'Lost property must be treated with respect and . . .'

Grasper   Yes, I know that, but did you read the section that says that luggage left in the airport must be returned to the owner immediately? Any airline company that does not seek to restore lost luggage to its owner within 12 hours will be liable to a heavy fine and imprisonment.

Boggles   But we haven't got a plane . . .

Grasper   Precisely! So if you will let me take the briefcase, I have several planes, if you remember?

Boggles   No! *[Holds on to briefcase]*

Vanya   You must let him take it, Boggles.

Boggles   But if we let him take it, he'll open it and look at the information and the specialist questions – you know he will. And then he's bound to pass the inspection and the BOGGLES FLYING COMPANY will be finished!

Vanya   But if you don't let him take it, you will be fined and have to go to prison, so the BFC will be finished anyway!

Boggles   Oh, Vanya, what shall we do? Grasper will win whatever we do!

Vanya   What does your heart say, Boggles? What would the Governor want you to do?

Boggles   I'm not sure, Vanya, I'm not sure.

Day 4: Dirty tricks from Grasper

Theme: Kingdom practice

Jesus said, 'If you love me, you will obey my commands.' (John 14:15)

Scene

Airport The FAST AIRLINE GROUP (FAG). Smart desk, stands next to the BOGGLES FLYING COMPANY (BFC) desk which is very shabby, untidy, with hand-written signs, etc.

Props list

FAG desk and sign As before.

Computer As before.

Passport processing machine As before.

Swivel chair As before.

Old table As before.

BFC sign As before.

Phone on Grasper's desk – could be a mobile.

Stepladder.

Pasting table.

Large paste brush.

Wallpaper A roll of old, thin paper will suffice.

Bucket of 'paste' This could be simply water, but if it could be thickened, it would 'behave' better. If additives are used, be careful in case the slapstick routine gets 'paste' in Boggles' eyes.

'Poison' paste box A large cereal box will do, covered with paper and a suitable label.

The play

The story so far (*possibly spoken by a narrator*)
Vanya, a citizen of Banandra, has arrived in the Governor's country. Boggles, a pilot who has set up his own airline – the BOGGLES FLYING COMPANY – has enabled Vanya to receive a passport from the Governor. Frederick Grasper, owner of the FAST AIRLINE GROUP, is trying his best to get Vanya sent back to her own country. Grasper has learned that there is to be a Government Inspection in the airport, and that the winning airline will receive a large sum of money invested in the company, but he is not telling Boggles.

Grasper is smart and calm behind his desk. Phone rings and he answers it.

Grasper   Good morning, Fast Airline Group, Frederick Grasper speaking. How may I help you? Oh, good morning, Mrs Farquason-Smythe. And how are you today? Yes, I am sorry to hear about the cake competition. I'm afraid it was that Boggles' fault. As I told you, I asked him especially to be careful about your cake, but he said he didn't care . . . Yes, I quite agree . . . he *is* a disgrace to the airport, but we know he will be finished when this inspection happens, and you can safely invest in FAG. Sorry? There will be some technical questions? What kind of technical questions? What? Worried? Me? No, of course not, dear lady, but thank you for the warning. I can look up the latest papers and things from the Governor . . . best to be prepared. By the way, I've suggested our friend Boggles does some decorating to smarten up his area of the airport. But have no fear . . . he will make such a mess that it will make the inspectors very unhappy, I'm sure . . . Yes, I quite agree. Thank you for ringing. Goodbye.

[Boggles enters, carrying paper and pasting table]

Boggles I've got everything, Grasper, except the paste – you said you'd get some?

Grasper Yes, and I've even had some mixed up for you. It will only cost you £5 for the whole lot – a great saving, I can assure you.

Boggles You're a real sport, Grasper. *[Gives Grasper £5]* I'll just get everything ready, if you could get the paste?

Grasper Certainly, dear boy. We don't want to hold you up, do we?

[Grasper exits to get paste, whilst Boggles has some difficulty erecting table, etc. After a while, Grasper returns with bucket of 'paste' and brush]

Grasper Here we are. Now, don't let me get in the way. *[Hands over bucket and sits at desk to work]*

Boggles Thanks again, Grasper.

[Next few minutes can be taken up by various slapstick decorating exercises . . . mismeasuring paper, trying to paste paper that keeps rolling up, walking up ladder through paper, etc. Ends up with Grasper roaring with laughter at Boggles' efforts. Vanya enters]

Vanya Boggles! What have you been doing?

Boggles I've been trying to improve our image, Vanya. It was Grasper's suggestion. *[Vanya and Grasper exchange glances]* It isn't as easy as it looks, though, Vanya.

Vanya Oh, Boggles! I'm sure you don't decorate an airport as you would a room in your house! I think that another try at our sign might be more effective!

Boggles Do you think so – oh, I suppose you're right.

Vanya I think so. *[Sniffs]* What is that smell, Boggles?

Boggles *[Sniffs his armpits]* It's not me . . . but I know what you mean, it's a strange smell, isn't it? I think it might be the wallpaper paste.

Vanya *[Smells the bucket]* You are right – it is not a good smell. Where did you get this, Boggles?

Boggles Well, Grasper got it for me on the cheap – only £5 the lot!

Vanya £5! In Banandra, wallpaper paste costs very little. *[Turns to Grasper]* What kind of wallpaper paste costs so much in your country, Mr Grasper? May I see it?

Grasper *[Annoyed at Vanya's interference]* It's got nothing to do with you, Miss Nosy-Parker. But if you must know, this is what Boggles has been using. *[Fetches box from off-stage]* This was developed by our country's scientists at great expense.

Vanya *[Takes box to examine it]* What is in it that smells so strange? *[Reads]* 'Highly Toxic. Do not use with bare hands. Developed as part of agricultural pest programme.'

Grasper *Pest* programme? I thought it said '*Paste* programme'! Here, give it to me. I'll throw the lot out – don't worry, Boggles, I won't charge you anything for this.

Boggles Hang on a minute. Isn't that part of the box of stuff that came in the other week? I thought it had specific instructions to dispose of it . . . Yes . . . that's right, I remember . . . there was an order written by the Governor himself saying that it had to be flown out to a special place where it would be safely destroyed. How come you've still got some?

Grasper Well, you know Government orders! They are so fussy about things. All that fuss over some boxes of powder. I happened to spill some, and when I saw there was nothing to be afraid of, I decided to keep it in case it came in handy.

Boggles How do you know there was nothing to be afraid of?

Grasper 'Cos it looks perfectly all right! I know it smells a bit, but it's a bit like medicine that tastes horrible, but is really good for you!

Vanya I think that was a bad mistake, Mr Grasper.

Boggles You're dead right there, Vanya! I might be dead, too! *[Takes box from Grasper]* The Governor wouldn't give an order just for the sake of it. He knows what is best for us and for the country. If this is poisonous, I might be affected!

Grasper Don't be stupid, Boggles! I tell you, the Governor only writes these things as *advice*, not rules! In my opinion, there is nothing wrong with that paste powder.

Boggles But it's not *paste* powder, is it? It's some kind of *pest* powder, used for killing some kind of bugs in fields and things.

Vanya   And it was not even considered safe for that – and that is why it was supposed to be destroyed!

Boggles   Rules are to be obeyed, Grasper, even if we don't agree, or even if we don't understand them. We must trust the Governor's wisdom on this – he only wants the best for us!

Grasper   Oh, if you're so worried, give it here. *[Takes box]* I'll put it in the dustbin, and I'll get some of my men to clean everything here, too!

Boggles   Thank you, Grasper, but putting it in the dustbin is not good enough! You just don't do that sort of thing in the Governor's country – and you know it. Unless you agree to take that and any other boxes you may have to the special place the Governor told you about, I'll have to report you.

Grasper   No, you mustn't do that – not before the inspection. We don't want any bad reports to affect things . . .

Boggles   Inspection? What inspection? What are you talking about?

Grasper   *[Annoyed at letting the information slip out]* I'm not saying – unless you agree not to report me for my mistake about this powder.

Vanya   I'm sure Boggles will not be so mean as long as you promise to dispose of the powder properly.

Boggles   If you agree, I agree !

Grasper   Because I know you'll keep your word, I'll tell you. I happen to know that there is to be a special inspection here at the airport sometime soon – including some very technical questions. But you'll never pass the inspection, and you know it. And so your stupid Flying Company will be finished! Ha ha! *[Walks off laughing, carrying box of powder]*

              [Boggles and Vanya look dismayed before they exit]

Day 5: Boggles is tempted

Theme: Kingdom choices

Jesus said, 'The Holy Spirit, the Spirit of truth . . . will guide you into truth.' (John 16:13, NIV)

Scene

Airport The FAST AIRLINE GROUP (FAG). Smart desk, stands next to the BOGGLES FLYING COMPANY (BFC) desk which is very shabby, untidy, with hand-written signs, etc.

Props list

FAG desk and sign, with computer, passport machine, swivel chair, Boggles' 'desk' and sign. All as before.

Briefcase This is specially rigged to 'explode' in the final episode. Use some gold paint to paint an official-looking 'crest' on the case. It could be a nice-looking box, instead.

Robotic processing machine A large box, suitably painted, large enough for Vanya to crouch inside unseen. Mount it on castors to make it easier to drag on stage. Paint it grey and make it look rather 'electro-mechanical'! It should have an 'input' slot, a large 'output' slot, and a hole through which VANYA can squirt water at GRASPER. Add some kind of 'speaking tube'.

Paper. For Boggles' trick on Grasper.

Envelope. For Boggles' trick on Grasper.

Glass of water (on FAG desk) For Boggles' trick on Grasper.

Water pistol (or garden spray). For Boggles' trick on Grasper.

Flowerpots (small and large). For Boggles' trick on Grasper.

Matchboxes (small and large). For Boggles' trick on Grasper.

Governor's handbook A large (red?) hard-backed book.

The play

The story so far *(possibly spoken by a narrator)*
Frederick Grasper, owner of the FAST AIRLINE GROUP, is trying his best to get rid of BOGGLES FLYING COMPANY and get Vanya sent back to her own country. Grasper has learned that there is to be a Government Inspection in the airport, and that the winning airline will receive a large sum of money invested in the company. He has told Boggles about the inspection, but not about the money. However, he thinks that the BOGGLES FLYING COMPANY will fail the inspection, but he would like to be sure.

Boggles is behind the desk, trying to work with papers and books. Grasper is smart and calm behind his desk.

Grasper   Just look at you! Boggles – I wouldn't even try, if I were you. You'll never pass the government inspection. You are a mockery of an airline! You have no planes, you have one employee – a highly unsuitable immigrant . . .

Boggles   I'll get a plane when I need one, don't you worry, Grasper. As I've said before, you may have all the smart machinery, but I have the friendly face that welcomes all to the Governor's country!

Grasper   Friendly face – pah! Listen, running an airline is serious business. Look, here I am with the latest computerised equipment for processing passports. All you have are a few pieces of paper and a pen . . .

Boggles   Don't you worry, Grasper. You won't be the only one with computerised equipment. I've had a special delivery of a new robotic processing machine, so there!

Grasper   A robotic processing machine? Just what is one of those? Oh, don't bother – you're dreaming again, aren't you?

[Exits, shaking his head in disbelief. Vanya enters carrying a briefcase – Boggles helps her – can experience some difficulty trying to get it onto the messy desk, etc.]

Boggles   What's this, Vanya? Some more of your luggage?

Vanya   No, I found it near the departure gate.

Boggles   Right. Well put it down and help me a minute.

[Exit while Grasper enters opposite side. After a few moments, Boggles enters dragging large box]

Grasper   What *have* you got there?

Boggles   I told you – it's my robotic processing machine.

Grasper   And what is it supposed to do?

Boggles   Just about anything. Look, it will type letters for me. *[Speaks into machine – machine makes noises, etc. Piece of paper comes out of slot, Grasper takes it and reads what Boggles dictated]*

Grasper   I don't believe it!

Boggles   It will even put the letter in an envelope and give it to me, ready to post! *[Puts paper into machine – out comes envelope]*

Grasper   Hmmm.

Boggles   It even enlarges things – look. *[Puts in small object – large object comes out – does this once or twice]*

Grasper   I see. *[Realising that he is being tricked]* Do you think it could enlarge a glass of water? *[Tips some water into machine but is squirted with a lot more! Boggles laughs as Grasper exits, and Vanya comes out of box laughing]*

Boggles   Vanya, that was great!

Vanya   It was fun, Boggles, but I hope it did not make Mr Grasper too angry.

Boggles   No – he'll get over it!

Vanya   Anyway, Boggles, what shall we do with this case I found? *[Picks up the briefcase]* Look – it has a special sign on it.

Boggles   That's a government crest. Vanya, this must belong to a government official. Where did you say you found it?

Vanya   By the departure gate. Whoever it belongs to must have flown out with FAG's morning flight an hour ago.

Boggles   Well, it can't be one of our flights – we still haven't got a plane!

Vanya   It looks very important.

Boggles   I wonder. Vanya, do you think it belongs to a government observer?

Vanya   What do you mean?

Boggles   I mean, what if a government observer has already been to the airport, you know, an advance look at things, ready for the inspection?

Vanya   Do you think so?

Boggles   I do – and that case may contain some important information about the inspection!

Vanya   What shall we do?

Boggles   We ought to return it to the owner, I guess. But I'd love to have just a little look inside. You know, that information could give us the edge over Grasper and FAG.

[Vanya produces large handbook]

Vanya   Let's see what the Handbook says . . .

Boggles   Oh, I know what it says . . .

Vanya   It says, 'Lost property must be treated with respect and confidence, as if it were still in the hands of the owner . . .'

Boggles   In other words, 'Hands off!' But still, I could just have a *little* look . . .

Vanya   No, Boggles. You know that would be against the Governor's wishes.

Boggles   Ah, but he isn't here, is he? And when the inspector comes . . .

[Grasper enters]

Grasper   . . . When the inspector comes he will see that FAG is the supreme airline, and that your poor excuse of a company will have to go!

[Vanya and Boggles groan and shake their heads]

Grasper   Hello, what have we here?

Vanya   It's some lost property.

Boggles   It's a government briefcase, Grasper, left by the departure gate.

Grasper   So I see . . .

Vanya   And Boggles thinks it may belong to an observer who's already come to look at the airport – a kind of advance inspection!

Grasper   Oh yes, I see what you mean. Well, if you let me take it, I can fly it over the mountains to Government House on the next flight.

Boggles   No – we'll just hang on to it for the moment.

Grasper   But you know what the handbook says?

Vanya   Yes, it says that 'Lost property must be treated with respect and . . .'

Grasper   Yes, I know that, but did you read the section that says that luggage left in the airport must be returned to the owner immediately? Any airline company that does not seek to restore lost luggage to its owner within 12 hours will be liable to a heavy fine and imprisonment.

Boggles   But we haven't got a plane . . .

Grasper   Precisely! So if you will let me take the briefcase, I have several planes, if you remember?

Boggles   No! *[Holds on to briefcase]*

Vanya   You must let him take it, Boggles.

Boggles   But if we let him take it, he'll open it and look at the information and look at the specialist questions – you know he will. And then he's bound to pass the inspection and the BOGGLES FLYING COMPANY will be finished!

Vanya   But if you don't let him take it, you will be fined and have to go to prison, so the BFC will be finished anyway!

Boggles   Oh, Vanya, what shall we do? Grasper will win whatever we do!

Vanya   What does your heart say, Boggles? What would the Governor want you to do?

Boggles   I'm not sure, Vanya, I'm not sure.

Day 6: All-age service: Grasper's narrow escape

Theme: Kingdom attitudes

Jesus said, 'You must go on growing in me and I will grow in you . . .'
(John 15:4, J.B. Phillips version)

Scene

As Day 2 – Airport The FAST AIRLINE GROUP (FAG). Smart desk, stands next to the BOGGLES FLYING COMPANY (BFC) desk which is very shabby, untidy, with hand-written signs, etc.

Props list

FAG desk and sign, with computer, passport machine, swivel chair, Boggles' 'desk' and sign All as before.

Tools

Briefcase or box As in previous day's episode. This is to be fitted with a theatrical miniature 'pot flash', a device that is set off by connecting a 9V battery. When GRASPER re-enters, pushing the briefcase, the wire could be connected, with someone ready to trigger the 'explosion' at the right moment. It is, of course, very important that no one is actually near the briefcase when the flash is set off. Whilst 'trying' to open it with his tools, GRASPER could actually open it an inch or two, and when he is pulled away the pot flash is triggered.

Medal This could simply be made from gold-coloured cardboard, and attached to a loop of red ribbon.

The play

The story so far *(narrator)*
Boggles, owner of the newly formed BOGGLES FLYING COMPANY, has welcomed Vanya, a citizen of Banandra, to the Governors' country. This has displeased Frederick Arthur Grasper, owner of the FAST AIRLINE GROUP, who claimed she was unsuitable for the Governor's country and should not have a passport. Vanya has found a briefcase, which they believe belongs to a government observer. They think this briefcase contains important information about an inspection that is due to take place in the airport, an inspection that will decide the fate of the BFC – the BOGGLES FLYING COMPANY.

Grasper is behind his desk. Boggles and Vanya enter, carrying the box/ briefcase, placing it on the BFC desk.

Grasper There you are, Boggles. Have you come to your senses yet? Are you going to let me take the briefcase back to Government House on my next plane?

Boggles   I have no choice, Grasper, and you know it!

Grasper   Oh, but you *do* have a choice, Boggles. Keep it much longer and I will have to report you. And then you will be in trouble – a large fine and a time in prison – and all because you would not let me take this briefcase back to where it belongs!

Vanya   But we know that if you take it, you will look in it first, and get the information about the inspection – and that will not be fair!

Grasper   As if I would do such a thing! Boggles, Miss Vanya, you have the wrong idea about me. I am simply a hard-working business man with an airline to run. I may seem hard and uncaring, but that is all a mask. Deep inside I am a deeply caring man. Trust me!

Boggles   I'd like to trust you, Grasper, but I know how wrong that would be.

Grasper   I am deeply hurt, Boggles. By the way, time is ticking on – Government House will be waiting for news of the lost luggage. Tell me, would it help if I promised to employ Miss Vanya if the BOGGLES FLYING COMPANY fails the inspection?

Vanya   But I don't want to work for him!

Boggles   But it might be for the best, Vanya. He might even give me my old job back!

Grasper   Don't push your luck, Boggles. Anyway, make your mind up.

Boggles   All right, Grasper. Take the briefcase back to Government House for me.

Grasper   What a sensible person you are, Boggles. Here, give it to me *[Takes the briefcase]* I won't let it out of my sight . . . *[Exit]*

Vanya   Why did you let him have the briefcase, Boggles?

Boggles   You heard him, Vanya. I really had no choice. I haven't any money to pay a large fine – and I certainly don't want to go to prison, just for hanging on to a briefcase that might have information to help the BFC to pass a government inspection! Besides, you'll be OK – now that you have your passport from the Governor, he'll keep his word and give you a job, I think.

Vanya   But what about you, Boggles, what will you do?

Boggles   I don't know. But everything will work out OK, you'll see. Hey, don't be so sad.

[Begins to sing and dance. At end, Vanya exits. Boggles leans on desk. Grasper enters, pushing briefcase on floor, he is carrying various tools]

What are you doing, Grasper? You said you were going to put the briefcase on the next flight across the mountains.

Grasper   Yes, I did, didn't I? Well, Boggles, this government inspection means too much for me. I'd like to win fair and square, but that's too risky. I want to be *sure* I'll win.

Boggles   But you promised.

Grasper   Yes, but I've changed my mind. You've got to be ruthless to survive in business, Boggles. You must understand that. 'Look after Number One' is my motto, and look where it's got me! You are just too soft, too nice, too honest. The world is no place for people like you, Boggles, I'm sorry! Now, if you'll excuse me, I've a bit of breaking and entering to do! Oh, and one more thing – I just telephoned Government House to say that you had the luggage and had refused to hand it over to me to bring back safely!

Boggles   But that's a lie!

Grasper   Yes, but it's your word against mine.

Boggles   And Vanya's.

Grasper   But they won't take the word of a citizen of Banandra, an illegal immigrant who has no proper job . . .

Boggles   You rotter!!!

[Grasper laughs and gets on with the job. Vanya enters]

Vanya   Boggles, what is the matter?

Boggles   It's Grasper. He doesn't mean to do anything he promised. I'm still going to be fined and go to prison, and I'm afraid you won't have a job, Vanya! Look, he's trying to open the briefcase now. He'll get the information he needs to pass the government inspection.

Vanya   But he mustn't interfere with the briefcase! *[She runs over and tries to pull Grasper away from the box. He resists, pushing her away violently]*

Boggles   What's the matter, Vanya?

Vanya   We've got to run – get away from here now, Boggles.

[She tries to pull Boggles off-stage]

Boggles   What's the matter, Vanya, what are you doing?

Vanya   It's the case, Boggles. It's booby-trapped to stop it getting into wrong hands. It will blow up soon after a wrong person tries to open it! Come on – we must get out of here!

Boggles   But Grasper – I can't let him get hurt. *[Runs over to Grasper – pulls him, struggling, off briefcase. As they get clear, briefcase explodes]*

Grasper   You fool, Boggles! Look what you've done now. We'll never know the information that the briefcase contained! But that won't save you! I'll make sure you never pass the government inspection!

Vanya   On the contrary, Mr Grasper. *[Vanya has lost her accent]* It is you who has failed the inspection.

Grasper   What do you mean?

Vanya   I am no foreign visitor. I am the assistant to the Governor himself. The Governor has been looking for someone who best reflects his nature, his interests. *[Turns to Boggles]* It is you, Captain Boggles, who is that someone. You were willing to deny yourself – even risking your life to save this man. In so many ways you reflected the nature of the Governor, and on his behalf I award you this medal. You will be an official airline of this country!

Grasper   I don't believe it!

Boggles   Neither do I, I think. But thank you, Vanya.

Grasper   I'm finished!

Boggles   What do you mean?

Grasper   All this equipment – I've spent everything I have on it all. I was relying on passing the inspection, because Mrs Farquason-Smythe told me there would be a large sum of money for the winning company!

Vanya   Do not worry, Mr Grasper. The Governor knows all about your situation. He has a plan to help you out. We feel there is room for two good airline companies, if you have truly learned your lesson. But now it's time for us all to celebrate!

THE END

PUPPET STORIES

Production notes

Puppets are a wonderful way of conveying biblical truth. They can either tell a Bible story in a simple straight fashion, or they can add a fun element. These scripts offer both approaches (though not for every story). Many people use the 'one way' style of puppet, which has a large mouth, and has one or both arms moved by an attachable rod. This is not the place for a treatise on puppetry, however. There are books specially dedicated to that purpose, if necessary.

We have some simple words of advice:

The scripts

Record the scripts, if possible, using the best voices you can get. Remember to leave enough empty spaces when the action is taking place. (Practical note: Beware recording equipment that has automatic level control. It will 'hunt' for a sound during the silences, which means a loud hissing sound.)

Music

Add appropriate music, if possible, as an introduction, and at the end. In some scripts, there may be occasions for music at other times, to denote the passage of time.

If you have someone with computer knowledge, they may be able to edit your recordings, to 'tidy them up'.

Day 1

Jesus the servant (John 13:2-17)

Cast

Peter, John, Jesus

[Peter and John enter]

Peter That was the most amazing Passover meal!

John The Master gave us a lot to think about.

Peter Where is he, by the way?

John Gone to wash his hands, probably – he said something about getting some water.

Peter We didn't spill anything on the table, did we? We only borrowed this room, and I suppose he wants to make sure we return it as good as we found it.

John Of course we'll return it – we can't take a room with us when we go, can we?

Peter *[Sarcastically]* Ha, ha – very funny. You know what I mean.

John Sorry, Peter. I was just trying to be funny. Oh – here's Jesus now – and he's carrying a bowl of water. *[Looking off-stage]*

Peter Perhaps we *did* spill something *[Looks around to see if food or drink was spilt]*

John No, Peter – it's not that – look what the Master is doing.

Peter He's kneeling down and taking Philip's sandals off . . . He's washing Philip's feet.

John Uuugh – *I* wouldn't do that, even if you paid me. His feet smell awful even when they're supposed to be clean! And he's been running around again – you never know what he's trodden in!

Peter Jesus is drying Philip's feet, too, with a towel. I don't understand – that's the servant's job – why is the Master doing it?

John Because we haven't got a servant, Peter! We're the disciples, perhaps we should be doing it.

Peter No – surely not. Hang on – Jesus is coming to us.

John Ho, ho – he's going to give the job to you!

Peter Oh no, surely not . . .

[Jesus enters, stand by Peter]

Jesus Peter, take your sandals off.

Peter Are you going to wash *my* feet, Master?

Jesus I know you don't understand what I'm doing, and why – but you will.

Peter   No, Lord, you're not going to wash my feet – it's not right . . .

Jesus   If I don't wash you, Peter, you can't be part of what I'm doing.

[Jesus bends to wash Peter's feet]

Peter   Then give a me wash all over – here – wash my hands . . . and my head . . . and my . . .

Jesus   Peter! You had a bath this morning – it's only your feet that need a wash now. There, that's you done. *[Stands]*   Now you, John . . .

John   If you must, Jesus.

Jesus   Yes, I must. *[Bends down to wash John's feet]*

Peter   This is so awful – Jesus is the Master – he's the last person to be washing his disciples' feet!

Jesus   *[Standing]* Listen, all of you. I *am* your Lord and Master, and I *have* washed your feet. If I can do it, so can you. This is the kind of way you show your love for others. Don't just listen to what I say – do it!

Day 2

The unforgiving servant

Cast

King, Smith, Jones

King	Now, I suppose you know why I've called you here today?
Smith	Er . . . to polish your boots, Your Majesty?
King	No.
Smith	Oh, er . . . to feed Your Majesty's royal dogs perhaps?
King	No.
Smith	Er . . . I know – to lend you some money?
King	NO! I am the king – why would I borrow money from you?
Smith	Of course not, Your Majesty.
King	But – you are partly right – you owe me some money.
Smith	Really? Do I? Oh dear.
King	Yes! Oh dear indeed. Do you know how much?
Smith	50 pence?
King	Try again.
Smith	£1?
King	£1000!
Smith	£1000! Are you sure? But, I'm broke . . . *[He grovels]* My wife's broke, my children are broke, the hamster's broke, we're all broke . . .
King	Oh, stop grovelling . . . stop grovelling, get up.
Smith	Yes, OK, sorry. But we'll never be able to pay you what we owe, Your Majesty. I'm really, really, really sorry.
King	All right then – only one thing for it. You don't have to pay me at all. I'll let you off the entire amount.
Smith	Wow! Really? Oh thank you. Thank you . . .
King	Yes, well, don't let it happen again.
Smith	I won't, Your Majesty. Goodbye. Hey! I'm a free man, *[He leaves]* I got away with it, I got away with it . . . *[Enter Jones. Smith sees him]* Hang on. Isn't that Jones over there. Hey – Jones, you owe me some money!
Jones	Oh no, do I? Oh dear! How much – £100?
Smith	No.

Jones   £200?

Smith   No.

Jones   Not £500?

Smith   NO! £5 – you owe me £5, I want it now.

Jones   But I can't – I'm broke, my wife's broke, my children are broke, the hamster's broke, we're all broke . . .

Smith   Oh don't give me those excuses. Right, you're going into prison until you pay it all back . . .

[He throws him off. The king re-enters and shouts his name]

Smith   Ah, Your Majesty! Hello, how are you?

King   I am not too good.

Smith   Oh dear. Not flu, I hope.

King   I have heard very bad things. Very, very bad things. I let you off £1000, so what did you do?

Smith   I was very grateful.

King   And?

Smith   And I went to tell everyone what a nice person you are.

King   No you didn't – I heard what you did – you threw Jones into prison for just £5.

Smith   Did I? Oh, that must have been a mistake. Are you sure it wasn't my brother? People are always getting us mixed up . . .

King   Quiet! I let you off – why didn't you forgive him for his debt . . . It's too late now. You don't have time to explain – you're off to prison.

Smith   Am I? What for? To visit Jones?

King   No – to replace him! Guards! Set Jones free and throw this man in jail. Come on, it's prison food for you . . .

[He drags Smith off by the scruff of the neck]

Copyright © Dave Hopwood

Day 3

The feast (Luke 14:18-23/Matthew 22:1-10)

Cast

Jo *(a servant)*, King, 2 or 3 guests *(or more if you have enough space, etc.)*

Props

Crown for king, toy laptop, phone, balloons

Music

Suitable pop music

King	*[Enters, looking around]* Where is he? *[Calls]* Jo! *[Louder]* Jo! Oh! he's never here when I want him. Jo!
	[Jo enters, whistling]
King	There you are.
Jo	Hi, boss.
King	Listen, I've had an idea. I want to give a huge banquet to celebrate my son's wedding. I'm going to ask all my friends. We'll have a band, a marquee, a bouncy castle and . . .
Jo	Hold it, hold it, boss. One thing at a time. When is this?
King	Next Saturday. Now, make a list of the guests. I'll ask the Beckhams, the Blairs, the Windsors and . . . let me see. Tell you what – I'll go and make a list of guests and you go and get some invitations done and sort out what we need. You could use the laptop computer.
	[Music as both exit. After a brief pause, Jo re-enters with laptop computer]
Jo	I've done the invitations, and sent them out. The king has asked far too many people if you ask me. Now what else? *[Looks at computer, checking list]* I've ordered the marquee, the band – tried to get S Club but couldn't – we'll have to make do with the local band, the 'Dischords'. Hope that's OK. Perhaps I'll ask Will or Gareth – or both!
	What's next? Ah – the caterers. They're arranged. I've asked the firm 'Really Tasty Food to Your Door'. We're having crisps, rolls, sausages, burgers, chicken nuggets, samosas, cheese dips, chips, jelly, ice cream, strawberries, cream, meringues, chocolate cakes, and sweets galore. It should be good. Now to fix a bouncy castle . . .
	[King enters]
King	Jo, Jo, what about hot-air balloon rides?

Jo	What about them?
King	It would be brill! Arrange it – look in the *Yellow Pages*.
	[Exit King in a hurry]
Jo	Oh no! Another thing to organise! This is over the top! *[Exit]*
	[Music]
Narrator	The day arrived. There was much coming and going in the palace . . .
	[Jo keeps appearing then disappearing, finally comes back with laptop]
Jo	*[Looking at computer]* Oh dear, the king won't like this, an e-mail from Mr and Mrs Brown. They can't come, something about buying a house in Spain and they've gone to see it . . .
	[Phone rings – Jo exits, comes back with phone]
	Hello. Yes. Yes. You've got a new car, a Mercedes . . . Well, can't you come in it? . . . No . . . you need to try it first. Um! So you're definitely not coming. The king will be sad. *[Puts phone down]* Oh dear. I don't think anyone is coming . . . all this food, too . . . Oh good, another e-mail. *[Looks at computer]* Oh bad, Sam Smith can't come either, he says he has just got married and gone on his honeymoon! OOOH! How do I tell the king?
	[King enters]
King	Hi, Jo. I'm so excited, we're ready. The band is here, the marquee is splendid. You made a good choice. I've had a go on the bouncy castle – such fun. I'm looking forward to the hot-air balloon ride. Er – you *did* arrange that, didn't you?
Jo	Yes, boss.
King	Now we just want a few guests. They're a bit late.
Jo	Well, I've had a few e-mails and phone calls, so far no one can come.
King	No one?
Jo	No one!
King	No one. Um! How dare they refuse? What shall we do?
	[King and Jo think. King jumps up and down angrily]
Jo	We could . . . no. *[pause]* We could . . . no.
King	I know what we'll do. Go out to the town and streets and villages. Invite everyone, everyone you see. Include the poor, the blind, disabled people, young, old, people from any country. Fill up my house, we'll have a ball! Go on, quick now!
	[Exit Jo and King – music]

Narrator So the servant went and brought lots of people back, but none of the original guests came at all. But those who came had a wonderful time. Jesus invites all of us to his banquet in the Kingdom of heaven.

[As music continues, King enters with Jo and some guests, dancing to the music – one guest could have a bandage, or an eye patch, etc. – the audience could be invited to dance as well.]

Day 4

The sorting time (Matthew 25:34-46)

Puppets

King, Lizzie, Danny, 4 other puppet people

[Danny, Lizzie and three other puppets are in line, rather nervous. After a short pause, a big, booming voice shouts 'NEXT!' One puppet exits]

Lizzie   Not long now.

Danny   No – sorting time has come.

Lizzie   I'm rather nervous – I'm not sure if I'm a sheep or a goat, Danny.

Danny   Well, I don't know about *you*, Lizzie, but I'm *bound* to be a sheep. I mean, I've lived a good life. Not *too* good you understand. I mean, I've told a white lie or two, but nothing serious.

Lizzie   I *tried* to do what is right, but I'm not sure.

Danny   Well, as long as you are sincere, that's all that matters. You know, you do what you think is best for you . . .

Lizzie   Can't you be sincerely wrong?

Danny   Naa. Of course you can't!

Lizzie   But what about the Bible? I was taught to live by the Bible – to do what it says, even if you didn't agree with it.

Danny   No one believes in the Bible any more – I mean, there are many holy books, aren't there? And who knows which one is right? Like I said, as long as you are sincere.

[The big, booming voice shouts 'NEXT!' Another exits. They shuffle along a bit.]

Danny   I did look around for a book that agreed with my opinions.

Lizzie   Oh? Did you find one?

Danny   No – but I found two that had bits that I agreed with.

Lizzie   I see. And did they make you happy?

Danny   Not really. That's why I did my best to 'Look after Number One'.

Lizzie   What do you mean?

Danny   I mean, I remembered the saying, 'God helps those who help themselves', so I helped myself as much as I could.

Lizzie   I thought we had to help those who can't help themselves.

Danny   My dad said there are always scroungers who are too lazy to do any proper work.

Lizzie	But there are also people who are genuinely poor . . . That's why I always put some of my pocket money away to give to those who needed help.
Danny	You're daft! I put pocket money away for *me* – it soon mounted up if I was careful. But you always were a sucker! You often gave stuff away, didn't you?
Lizzie	Well I sort of thought I could do without, if it helped some-one worse off than me.
Danny	Well, *I* thought there were always people worse off, so why bother?
	[The big, booming voice shouts 'NEXT!' Another exits. They shuffle along a bit.]
Lizzie	You did very well at school, didn't you?
Danny	Of course! I always did well at exams 'cos I copied other people's work.
Lizzie	But that's cheating!
Danny	No it's not – I call it 'helping myself'. Listen, didn't the Lord even talk about 'loving ourselves'?
Lizzie	Yes . . .
Danny	Well, there you are. I reckon he meant us to be really happy and not get upset. I mean I couldn't do what you did.
Lizzie	What do you mean?
Danny	I mean you visited that old lady down the street, didn't you?
Lizzie	Mrs Tinker?
Danny	Mrs Stinker more like! Cor – she smelt awful – always did, my dad used to say.
Lizzie	But she was old and very ill – she needed someone just to keep her company.
Danny	But the smell! She must have been really dirty. And I bet she rambled on and on about the old days, about when she was a little girl.
Lizzie	Well, yes, but she just wanted someone to be there.
Danny	And where did it get you? She never left anything in her will for you, did she? It was a waste of time.
Lizzie	But that's not the point!
Danny	But it wasn't 'helping yourself' was it?
	[The big, booming voice shouts 'NEXT!' Another exits. They shuffle along a bit. There are just Lizzie and Danny left.]
Lizzie	We're next . . .

Danny   *I'm* next! Us sheep are more important than goats. Like I said, you've got to 'Look after Number One' if you're going to succeed. I mean – look at you! What have you done with your life? You've got nothing to show for it! I've got money in the bank, a nice big house, a big car . . .

[The big, booming voice shouts 'NEXT!']

Danny   Right. My turn! I hope you do well in the sorting – I'll put in a good word for you, if I can.

[Danny exits, leaving Lizzie alone. Off-stage, Danny's voice is heard . . . 'A goat? Me, a goat? You must be joking! That's not fair!' There is a pause, then King enters.]

King   Hello, Lizzie.

Lizzie   Hello. Is Danny a goat as well? We both got it wrong, then . . .

King   You didn't get it wrong, Lizzie. You're not a goat.

Lizzie   I'm not? But I wasn't very successful – I didn't *do* much with my life . . .

King   But you did, Lizzie. All those things you did – the money and things you gave away, the way you spent time with Mrs Tinker – when you did them for others, you did them for me. You tried to live by doing the things I said. That's why you're a sheep. Come on. I have some good things for you . . .

[Both exit]

Copyright © Capt Alan J. Price, CA

Day 5

Peter and Cornelius (Good news for everyone)

Cast

Cornelius, Angel, Simon Peter (possibly others – friends of Peter)

Cornelius	Three o'clock and it's time to pray! Coo – life is busy – praying to God, looking after some of the poor people – trying to run a Roman Legion – all those soldiers. Anyway . . . Dear Lord, it's me again, Captain Cornelius. I want to thank you . . .
	[There is a kind of mini-fanfare and the angel appears]
	Oo-er who are you? You're not God . . .
Angel	No, but he has sent me to have a word with you.
Cornelius	But I've prayed regularly – and all my family do, too. And we really try to help the poor people here in town. You know, give a little money, take round some food . . .
Angel	No, Cornelius, you're not in trouble. Listen – God has heard your prayers – he knows you're a kind man . . .
Cornelius	Thank you very much. I do try hard.
Angel	Be quiet and let me finish . . .
Cornelius	Sorry.
Angel	Quiet.
Cornelius	Yes – sorry.
Angel	As I was saying . . . God has heard your prayers. Send three of our men to the town of Joppa . . .
Cornelius	That's not too far away . . .
Angel	*Please* be quiet and let me finish.
Cornelius	Sorry.
Angel	Quiet!
Cornelius	Sorry!
Angel	Send three men to Joppa, to Simon's house near the sea, and find the other Simon.
Cornelius	Two Simons? How will they know which is which?
Angel	'Cos one owns the house, and he makes things with leather, and the other is called Simon Peter. He's staying as a guest of the other Simon.
Cornelius	How confusing. Will they have name badges?
Angel	No – they won't have name badges. Don't be silly. You're being very silly for a centurion.

Cornelius	Well, I don't often have angels appearing on my roof!
Angel	Anyway, ask Simon to come here to Caesarea.
Cornelius	Which one – the one who owns the house or the one who's staying there?
Angel	The one who's staying there – Simon Peter.
Cornelius	Right.
Angel	Good. I'm off, back to heaven – don't get them mixed up, will you?
Cornelius	No sir – I won't be a silly centurion.

[Angel exits, perhaps with another mini-fanfare. Cornelius shouts orders off-stage as he exits]

Right! You three. Get yourselves ready. You're going to Joppa . . .

Narrator	Four days later, the three soldiers returned to Captain Cornelius with Simon Peter and a few other men. Cornelius was waiting for them – and he had invited other guests to meet the man God wanted Cornelius to meet.

[Cornelius and Peter enter, possibly with others]

Cornelius	Do come in, your holiness. *[Bows to Peter]* I'm so humbled to have you here . . .
Peter	Don't bow to me – I'm just a man like you.
Cornelius	But God sent his angel to tell me to fetch you.
Peter	So your men told me. Listen, I never thought I'd be here in your house.
Cornelius	I know – you thought you'd be enjoying your holiday with the other Simon . . .
Peter	No, I mean I'm not supposed to be here. I'm a Jew, and Jewish people are not supposed to go into the homes of people who aren't Jews.
Cornelius	So why are you here? Why has God sent you?
Peter	A few days ago I was on the roof of Simon's house praying, just like you . . .
Cornelius	And God sent an angel to you, too?
Peter	No – I had a kind of dream – a vision – and I saw this large sheet come down from heaven. It had all kinds of animals, birds and reptiles – you know, snakes and things.
Cornelius	Strange!
Peter	What was even more strange was that I heard a voice – and I knew it was God speaking to me.
Cornelius	What did it say?
Peter	It said, 'Get up, Peter! Kill them and eat them.'

Cornelius	No!
Peter	Yes!
Cornelius	No!
Peter	Yes! And me, being a good Jewish man, said 'No, Lord!' I mean, we Jews have strict rules about what we can eat and what we can't. I couldn't break God's rules.
Cornelius	So what happened?
Peter	God said, 'If I allow it, then it is right.' And you know I had the same vision twice more. Then your men arrived and told me about the angel visiting you and here I am.
Cornelius	Won't you get into trouble?
Peter	Possibly. I had to make a choice – do I break the rules I've lived by all my life? But I knew that was what God was telling me. If he allows it, then it is right. It was not about food – it was about God's love being for everyone, not just for Jewish people. He loves and accepts anyone who worships him and lives a life that pleases him.
Cornelius	Wow – this is great! Come and tell my family and friends.
Peter	Certainly . . . I don't know if you have heard about the Lord Jesus. He is God's Son, and God sent him to teach us about God, and to die and come alive again . . . *[Exit as they talk]*

Copyright © Capt Alan J. Price, CA

Day 6 (Family service)

The soil and the seed

Cast

Two seeds *(in appearance these should be two large balls, with eyes and a mouth)*

1 Hello – nice here, isn't it?

2 Yep!

1 Been here long?

2 Nope!

1 You don't say much, do you?

2 Nope!

1 Come on – say a bit more than that, otherwise this sketch is going to last an awful long time!

2 OK.

1 That's better. So, where are we?

2 We're in the ground.

1 In the ground?

2 Yes – lovely, isn't it?

1 It could be worse, I suppose. We could be like my friend Harry.

2 Why, what happened to him?

1 Cor – it was awful! He was with a few of the other seeds when the farmer grabbed him and threw him out of the bag.

2 Well, that's what's supposed to happen to seeds, isn't it? The farmer throws us out onto the soil and we sink down and wait.

1 But Harry landed on the path around the edge of the field. He wasn't there long, though.

2 Why, what happened to him then?

1 The birds came along, and Harry ended up as a bird's dinner!

2 Poor Harry!

1 It could be worse.

2 What could be worse than that?

1 You could be like Emily.

2 What happened to Emily?

1 Well, the Farmer grabbed her and a few of the others and threw her out, too!

2 But she didn't land on the path?

1	No, she landed in a nice sunny place.
2	Lovely!
1	No it wasn't.
2	It wasn't?
1	No – at first it was all right. Emily sank into the ground and soon began to grow.
2	But that's good.
1	Yes, but it didn't last.
2	Why not?
1	I told you it was sunny.
2	Yes.
1	Well, Emily got very thirsty – *very* thirsty, because the sun was hot and the soil was drying out. But the ground was so stony that she couldn't get her roots down to where the moisture was, and she died.
2	Poor Emily!
1	But it could be worse!
2	What could be worse than being gobbled up by birds or being dried up on stony soil?
1	You could be like Sammy.
2	What happened to Sammy?
1	It was so sad.
2	It was sad for Harry and Emily!
1	Sammy landed in nice, warm soil.
2	But it was stony, right?
1	No, it was nice.
2	But you said it was worse!
1	It was – Sammy began to grow.
2	That's good!
1	But he wasn't alone.
2	That's good, too, isn't it, having company as a young growing plant?
1	Not that kind of company. You see, Sammy landed amongst the weeds and the thistles, and they are greedy. They want all the moisture, all the light, all the good things that a plant needs.
2	Oh dear!
1	Exactly! Sammy tried his best, he grew for a while, but soon he was dead, too, choked by those weeds and thistles.

2 The Farmer isn't doing too well, is he? I mean if his seeds don't land in good soil, with plenty of moisture, and room to grow, he won't get a good crop of wheat to get more seeds to make flour, or to plant to make more seeds . . .

1 That's why it's good we're here. I think we'll do well here.

2 I once heard a teacher say that the truth about God is like seeds that fell in different kinds of soil.

1 Did you?

2 Yes. The hard path has no place for the truth about God. It's like people who hear about God, but it doesn't go deep inside them. They don't want to change and it's like birds that come and take the truth away, as if the people had never heard it!

1 Not good.

2 No – and the stony soil is like people who receive the truth about God but don't get too serious about it – don't get *too* religious – you know, they don't go to church too much and don't read the Bible or anything.

1 Is that bad?

2 Well, it's sad. The teacher said that when things get hard, they don't know enough about God's truth, and their faith dies, too!

1 Sad.

2 Very sad. And that soil with the weeds and thistles . . .

1 I can guess – it's like people who receive the truth about God, but let other things choke it out – other things that become more important than God.

2 Right! People should be like this soil, with plenty of moisture and room to grow, letting God's truth go deep inside, so they can survive the bad times, and not letting anything else squash their love for God. Then they'll be fruitful, like us! Oooh.

1 What's up?

2 It's all right – I can feel a root coming out. Let's get on with the growing, shall we?

1 Right – I'm sure I'm beginning to swell a bit too . . .

SMALL-GROUP WORKSHEETS

Greens, Day 1: Kingdom love

Jesus showed his love by being like a servant

What did Jesus wash?
Colour the correct
picture.

Can you remember the verse?

Fill in the missing words . . .

John 15:12	Here	is	
Command.		each	other
just	as	I	have
	you.		

Reds, Day 1: Kingdom love

Unscramble these words and write in the footprints in the right order.

uyo rehe ym ovle htero aveh I dveol si ujts
amomdnc cahe sa Jhno 15:12

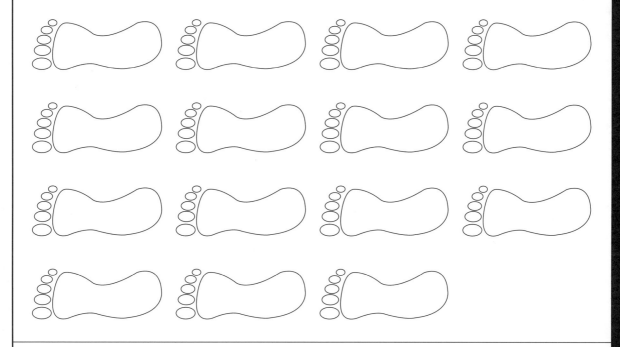

Jesus took the servant's role and washed the disciples feet.
How could you 'serve' other people?
Write your answer here:

_____

_____

Greens, Day 2: Kingdom justice

The story of the unforgiving servant

Can you spot 5 differences between these two pictures?

Jesus told this story because he wants us to know that he forgives us and that he wants us to forgive others.

Write a prayer in the speech bubble below, saying sorry to Jesus for the things you have done wrong and asking him to help you forgive others who have hurt you.

Reds, Day 2: Kingdom justice

The story of the unforgiving servant
(Matthew 18:21-35)

Complete these pictures to draw a cartoon version of the story.

Jesus told this story because he wants us to know that he forgives us and that he wants us to forgive others.

Write a prayer in the speech bubble here, saying sorry to Jesus for the things you have done wrong and asking him to help you forgive others who have hurt you.

Greens, Day 3: Kingdom living

Jesus invites us to his feast.
Can you set this table with lots of good things for a feast?

In our story, lots of people made excuses.
Are you going to accept his invitation and follow him?

You may like to write your reply to Jesus in this RSVP.

You are invited by his Majesty to be his Special Friend

RSVP:

Reds, Day 3: Kingdom living

The Banquet

In the story Jesus told, people made excuses
as to why they could not come.
What were these? Look up Luke 14:15-24.

1.

2.

3.

What excuses do people make today?

Jesus said he came to give us what?
Can you decode this verse and find out?

ylluf ti evah dna efil evah dluow enoyreve that os emac I dias suseJ.

Are you making excuses?
Or are you going to accept his invitation and follow him?

You may like to write your reply to Jesus in this invitation.

You are invited by his Majesty   to be his Special Friend.

RSVP:

Greens, Day 4: Kingdom practices

Jesus taught about helping people in need.
Match the word to the picture.

lonely   *hungry*   *sick*   *prison*   *thirsty*   *naked*

When we help others, it is like helping Jesus.
How can you help others? Draw in the boxes.

At home	*At school*	*With friends*

Prayer

Thank you Jesus for promising to send your Holy Spirit to help us.
Amen.

Reds, Day 4: Kingdom practices

Can you find these words from Matthew 25:31-46?

C	B	R	R	K	V	C	R	E	A	T	E	D	G	U	P	I	X
O	L	L	I	I	I	X	D	N	B	L	C	L	O	T	H	E	S
P	E	M	G	N	S	K	C	J	D	R	M	D	A	A	J	Q	J
N	S	R	H	G	I	I	Y	C	A	R	E	I	T	S	I	C	K
H	S	J	T	D	T	W	T	S	J	O	J	D	S	K	F	N	A
U	E	J	V	O	E	T	H	I	R	S	T	Y	K	S	S	V	P
R	D	G	Q	M	D	S	H	E	E	P	S	P	Z	H	V	E	R
P	E	A	T	S	T	R	A	N	G	E	R	E	D	B	K	T	E
K	V	C	D	R	I	N	K	B	A	W	G	L	N	C	Q	B	P
W	C	J	E	P	M	G	C	W	L	H	O	L	M	A	H	R	A
X	T	P	A	I	H	U	N	G	R	Y	J	R	E	V	K	U	R
A	Y	P	U	I	V	M	P	S	Z	R	P	N	L	F	M	E	E
W	H	Z	Z	Z	L	E	P	E	O	P	L	E	Q	D	T	H	D
T	D	G	K	Z	G	Q	H	W	E	L	C	O	M	E	D	I	W

sheep	hungry	naked	did
goats	eat	clothes	people
right	thirsty	sick	prepared
left	drink	care	created
receive	stranger	jail	world
kingdom	welcomed	visited	blessed

How can you help others?

At school_____

At home_____

With friends _____

Prayer

Thank you Jesus for promising to send your Holy Spirit to help us.
Amen.

Greens, Day 5: Kingdom choices

Which way should these men go to find Peter on the roof?
Can you help them through the maze?

THE HOLY SPIRIT SHOWS WHAT IS TRUE, AND WILL COME AND GUIDE YOU INTO THE FULL TRUTH. JOHN 14:15

God showed Peter through his dream that he wanted him to tell people from other countries about Jesus.
What did Peter see in his dream? Draw lots of the animals on this sheet.

Good news

Peter had to choose to obey God. Because he obeyed, people all over the world have heard about Jesus – including us.

Write a prayer, asking Jesus to help you choose his way.

Reds, Day 5: Kingdom choices

Work out these clues for this crossword.

ACROSS: 5. Who went to sleep on the roof? 6. A four-legged creature
7. Creatures that have no legs 8. When you sleep, sometimes you ....

DOWN: 1. Peter was staying here 2. The name of the man who sent for Peter
3. How many times did the sheet come down in Peter's dream?
4. Who told Cornelius about Peter?

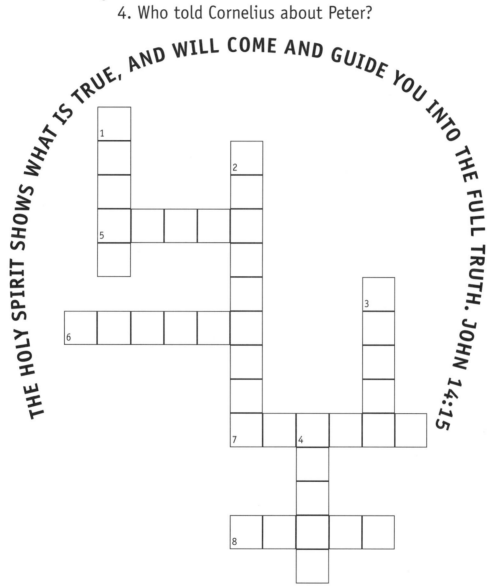

THE HOLY SPIRIT SHOWS WHAT IS TRUE, AND WILL COME AND GUIDE YOU INTO THE FULL TRUTH. JOHN 14:15

Good news

Peter had to choose to obey God. Because he obeyed,
people all over the world have heard about Jesus – including us.

Write a prayer, asking Jesus to help you choose his way.

APPENDICES

Appendix 1

Badge design

This may be used for a badge machine, or simply as an *Up, Up, Up and Away* logo. There are companies which will put this design on embossed plastic badges, but the cost is most effective when large quantities are ordered.

Appendix 2

Air traffic control:
Circle/diamond/square/star cards

These cards are used in the 'Air traffic control' team game. They can be enlarged and printed onto card. Draw the appropriate symbol on the other side of the cards.

Hint In using these cards, it may sometimes be an idea to 'cheat' a little in order to ensure the gap between the teams does not become too great. This means, for instance, saying the team has only to go back *one* space, when the card actually says *two*, etc. If this goes against your conscience, I suggest you don't print the actual values (1, 2, etc.) and spontaneously say the amount the team should move forward or back, etc.

Circle air traffic control cards

No wind to
hinder progress

GO FORWARD 2

Light load enables
faster airspeed

GO FORWARD 1

Late delivery
of in-flight
refreshments

STAY WHERE
YOU ARE

Control Tower clear
you for early
take-off

GO FORWARD 2

A strong
tailwind means
greater airspeed

GO FORWARD 3

New
experimental
fuel gives you
extra speed

GO FORWARD 1

Busy airspace
means delay in
landing

STAY WHERE
YOU ARE

Fewer passengers
means less fuel and
less weight

GO FORWARD 1

Diamond air traffic control cards

Take on
fresh fuel

GO FORWARD 1

Flight
attendants
on strike

GO BACK 1

Luggage
labels are mixed up

STAY WHERE
YOU ARE

Pilot
has overslept

STAY WHERE
YOU ARE

A tailwind
helps you

GO FORWARD 2

Ice on
the runway

TRY AGAIN

Minor
fault causes
delay in take-off

STAY WHERE
YOU ARE

Computer error in
navigation system

GO BACK 2

Square air traffic control cards

Forgotten a
passenger

GO BACK 1

Fuel level is low,
return to last airport

GO BACK 2

Another aircraft
in the vicinity

STAY WHERE
YOU ARE

Pilot has left
flight destination
behind

GO BACK 2

Bad weather ahead,
take evasive flight
path

GO BACK 2

Overshot end
of runway

GO BACK 1

Incoming flights
delay take-off

STAY WHERE YOU ARE

Turbulence –
reduce airspeed

GO BACK 1

Star air traffic control cards

What runs but has
no legs?
(Water or a train)

GO FORWARD 1

Make a paper plane
and throw it so it flies
into a bucket
4 metres away

GO FORWARD 3

Give a dancing
demonstration

GO FORWARD 1 OR 2

A 747 is better known as
what kind of jet plane?
(A 'Jumbo')

GO FORWARD 2

Whistle the
theme song

GO FORWARD 2

Draw a picture of a
helicopter

GO FORWARD 1

Blindfolded,
draw a picture of
a plane

GO FORWARD 3

Catch three wet sponges

GO FORWARD 3

Appendix 3

Sample team application form

This gives suggestions for the information to be given to team applicants, a procedure for Police Checking, and the actual application. Print this so that the applicant can keep the information, whilst handing in the application.

Up, Up, Up and Away Holiday Club

This is a holiday club run by Christians from the local churches. We aim to introduce the children to God in the person of Jesus Christ, to explore the Bible with them, and to help them look to Jesus as their special friend. Some children will already follow Jesus, and we aim to encourage them in their Christian Journey.

There are many different roles to be filled to make the event go well. The biggest number of team members will be **Small-group Leaders**, who will work with a group of 8-12 children, possibly with a helper. Please indicate overleaf which role you would prefer.

Team Members are required to:

1. Attend the Team Preparation Day/Sessions on *(date)*.
2. Do any necessary preparations for their role before the event.
3. Attend the daily team meeting for prayer and preparation at *(time)*.
4. Wear the badge/shirt etc., that identifies them as a team member during the event.
5. Act responsibly with the children, with no behaviour or language that will abuse a child or compromise the Christian message being taught.
6. Be aware that their actions are open to misinterpretation and therefore great care should be taken to avoid situations in which they could be misunderstood.

Team members can expect:

1. The full support of the Holiday Club organisers in the task before them.
2. To have no unreasonable demands made on them.
3. The prayerful support of others.
4. Craft materials and basic tools to be provided.

To comply with the Children's Act 1989, and to honour the children in our charge, each team member needs to complete and sign the declaration below, which must be handed to the Holiday Club organiser before the event.

In addition, if you wish to have a role which gives you unsupervised contact with children, you must be checked by the **Criminal Records Bureau**. If you have already been police-checked for work with children and young people, complete the appropriate boxes. For others, you will be told the procedure to follow.

GOOD PRACTICE GUIDELINES

- You should never be on your own in an unsupervised situation with a child or young person.
- You should never meet with a child or young person outside the organised activity without another worker being present.
- You will be responsible for ensuring that abusive peer activities do not occur, i.e. bullying, etc.
- All steps must be taken to ensure the venue is safe for children and young people and any concerns must be reported to the Team Leader who will then deal with the situation from there.

Team application (18 years +)

NAME..

ADDRESS ....

.... POST CODE ....

TELEPHONE ....

E-MAIL..

CHURCH ATTENDED ....

....

Your preferred role in the Holiday Club (please tick):

Small-group Leader	☐	Admin	☐
Small-group Helper	☐	First Aid	☐
Craft Team	☐	Technical (PA, etc.)	☐
Games Team	☐	Registration/Sales	☐
Drama Team	☐	Refreshments	☐
Music team	☐	Prayer Support	☐
Site and Equipment	☐	Steward/Security	☐

Previous experience Please give details of any other previous experience of looking after or working with children:

....

....

Relevant skills Briefly list any qualifications or skills appropriate to the role for which you are applying:

....

....

References Please provide the name and address of two people who have known you for at least two years, and who could provide a brief personal reference:

NAME..

ADDRESS ....

.... POST CODE ....

NAME..

ADDRESS ....

.... POST CODE ....

I would like to help in the Holiday Club. I understand that this is a Christian activity and am happy to participate on that basis. The information I have given on this form is true to be best of my knowledge.

SIGNED .... DATE ....

CHILDREN'S ACT 1989: CONFIDENTIAL DECLARATION

If you have been POLICE-CHECKED for work with children and young people, please give DATE and details of the ORGANISATION that requested that check. You do not need to complete Sections 1-6 following – please complete the remainder of the Application Form.

Date of Police Check	Organisation

If you have **NOT** been police-checked, please complete Sections 1-6 following:

1. Have you any health problem(s) which might affect your work with children or young people under the age of 18?   YES / NO

   If YES, please give details (use a separate sheet if necessary)

2. Have you since the age of 18, ever been known by any name other than the one given on this form (e.g. maiden name)?   YES / NO

   If YES, please give details (use a separate sheet if necessary)

3. Have you, during the past five years, had any home address other than that given on this form?   YES / NO

   If YES, please give details (use a separate sheet if necessary)

4. Has a child in your care, of for whom you have or had parental responsibility, ever been removed from your care, been placed on the Child Protection Register, or been the subject of a care order, a child assessment order, or an emergency protection order under the Children Act 1989, or a similar order under other legislation?   YES / NO

   If YES, please give details (use a separate sheet if necessary)

5a. Have you ever been convicted of any criminal offence?*   YES / NO

5b. Have you been cautioned by the police or bound over to keep the peace?   YES / NO

5c. Have you ever been found by a court exercising civil jurisdiction (including matrimonial or family jurisdiction) to have caused significant harm** to a child or young person under the age of 17 years? Or has any such court made any order against you on the basis of any finding or allegation that any child or young person was at risk of significant harm** from you?   YES / NO

   If you have answered YES to any question above, please give full details on a separate sheet.

* This question covers all convictions that are not spent under the Rehabilitation of Offenders Act 1974. It also covers 'spent' convictions if they relate to neglect, harm or abuse of children.
** 'Significant harm' means ill-treatment of any kind (including sexual abuse), or impairment of physical or mental health or development.

6. Has your conduct ever caused, or been likely to cause significant harm** to a child or young person under the age of 18, or put a child or young person at risk of significant harm, or to your knowledge has it ever been alleged that your conduct has resulted in any of those things?
   (This question relates to any conduct, whether in a paid capacity, as a voluntary worker or otherwise.)   YES / NO

   If YES, please give full details on a separate sheet, including the date(s) and nature of the conduct or alleged conduct, and whether you were dismissed, disciplined, moved to other work or resigned from any paid or voluntary work as a result.

Signed:... Date:...........................
Full Name: (PRINT)

PLEASE RETURN THIS SECTION TO THE HOLIDAY CLUB ORGANISER

Appendix 4: Theme song

UP, UP, UP AND AWAY

Capt. Alan Price, CA
arr. Gillian Venton

Appendix 5

The 'Magic washing machine' (Day 2)

You can make this box to your own dimensions. These are given for guidance only. You will need to experiment about the size of the pieces of cloth which will be hidden by the flap. Obviously, the bigger the box, the bigger the piece of cloth that can be hidden. Don't make it so big that you can't handle it easily, however.

Using a piece of card, make a tube, measuring 10cm x 10cm, around 15cm long. Paint the inside with black emulsion paint. Make a base 10cm x 10cm to fit snugly in the tube. Make a 'secret' flap, measuring 10cm x 13cm. Paint them both with the black paint (the flap should be painted on both sides).

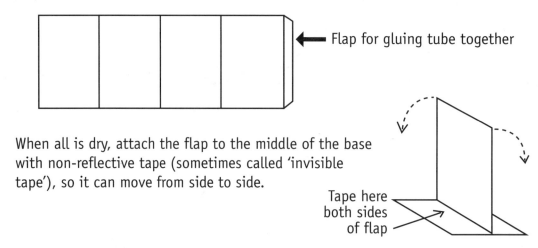

← Flap for gluing tube together

When all is dry, attach the flap to the middle of the base with non-reflective tape (sometimes called 'invisible tape'), so it can move from side to side.

Tape here both sides of flap

Insert the base, fixing it with glue or more tape. You could use a piece of velcro at the top of one side of the flap, with the matching piece stuck to the side of the tube. This means you could actually tip the box over and the hidden (spoilt) piece of cloth would not fall out.

If using velcro-type fastening, attach here

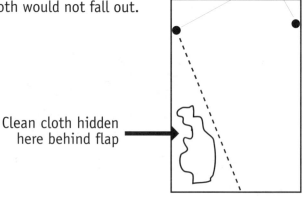

Clean cloth hidden here behind flap →

Most washing machines are white, and so you could paint it white outside, perhaps with the words 'Washing Machine' printed on it. To save painting, you could make this with black coloured card, covering the outside with white paper, with the words printed by a computer.

Start with the clean piece of cloth hidden under the flap (not the side with the velcro fastening). Be careful not to tip the box and operate the flap before you are ready, especially if you have used the velcro fastening. When you are ready to produce the 'cleaned' cloth, drop the dirty one in (pushing it down a little, if necessary) and tip the box until the flap goes over. Practise the handling of the box to get it right, before 'performing' the trick. One final hint: think of some way to put the 'washing machine' away, or hang on to it so that children don't get hold of it and see how the trick is done (though of course, many will work it out anyway!).

Appendix 6

Maze puzzle (Day 5)

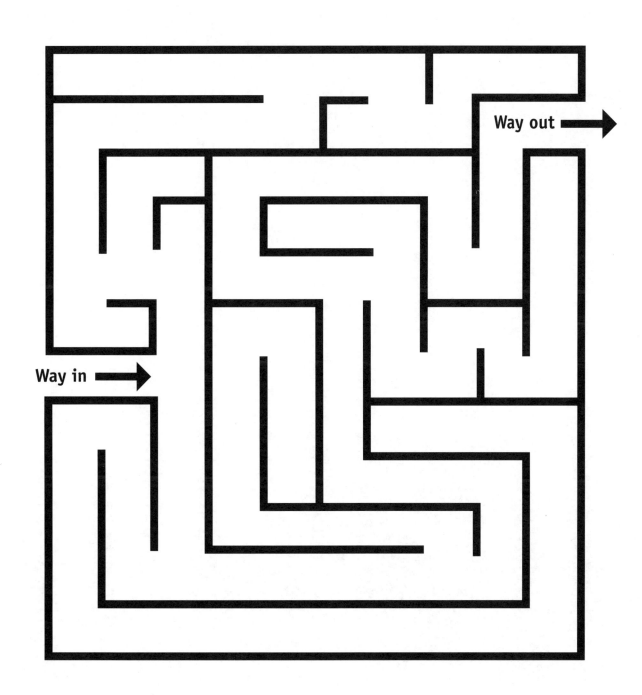

ACETATE MASTERS

Up, Up, Up and Away
(Theme prayer)

Father, thank you for sending
Jesus to show your love for
us, and your plan for our lives.

Through the Holy Spirit, help us
to 'take off' as we follow Jesus,
and to enjoy the adventure of faith.
In Jesus' name we pray. Amen.

Theme song (words)

Up, Up, Up and Away

Up, up, up and away,
we're taking off as we follow Jesus.
Up, up, up and away,
we're moving on with God.

Our luggage packed
and our ticket in hand,
we come to Jesus and we understand
that he paid a great price,
even willing to die;
when we know we're forgiven,
it's as if we can fly.

His Spirit's fuel
gives the power we need
for ev'ry word and for ev'ry deed;
and a beacon is there
to guide us along,
his Word in the Bible
shows what's right and what's wrong!

Words & Music Capt Alan J. Price, CA
Copyright © 1996 Daybreak Music Ltd
Silverdale Road, Eastbourne, East Sussex BN20 7AB

Scoreboard

Copy this onto OHP acetate, or onto a large sheet of hardboard. Use the plane shapes as score indicators. If on hardboard, you may like to have bulbs that light up as a plane 'lands'.

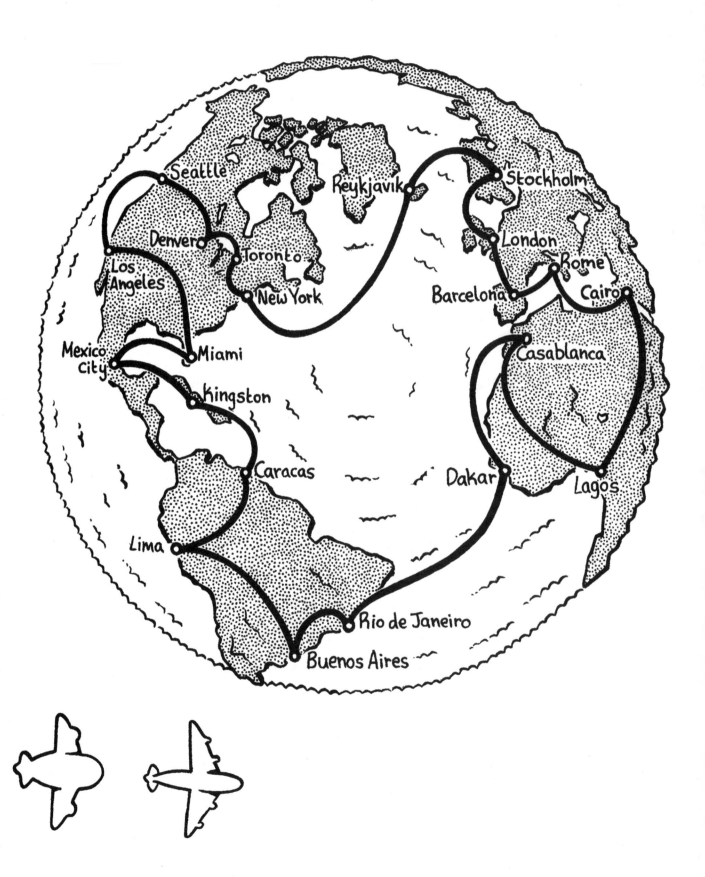